Signs of Pride

Wisconsin Towns and Their Claims to Fame

by

Callen Harty

ISBN: 9798394282263

DEDICATION

To my longest-lasting friend, Brian Doyle, whom I met when we were five years old. Thank you for being such an important part of my life.

ACKNOWLEDGMENTS

I would like to thank the following, without whom this book would not have been possible: Jackie Baker, Querida Lu Ahn Funck, Randi Johnson Hanson, Ralph Luedtke, Lauren Sheridan, Brian Wild, John Willems Van Dijk.

Cover photos by Callen Harty. Top left: World's Largest Badger, Birnamwood. Top right: Dr. Evermor's Forevertron, Sumpter. Middle: World's Largest Man-Made M, Platteville. Bottom left: Troll, Mount Horeb. Bottom center: Jimmy the Groundhog, Sun Prairie. Bottom right: World's Largest Corkscrew, Hurley.

Back cover photo of the author by Melody Harrison Hanson; used with permission.

PREFACE:

When I was still fairly young I noticed that it seemed like almost every Wisconsin town had a sign at its border proclaiming it to be the capital or home of something especially important to the citizens of that town. It is not unique to Wisconsin. Casey, Illinois, for example, has a dozen of the world's largest items, including a pencil, mailbox, and mouse trap. But Wisconsin does seem to have an overabundance of them. I have been keeping a list of these for years and decided that it would make an interesting book for those who are as fascinated with the state and these oddities as I am. A good number of them were listed on my personal website for a number of years. Numerous people have e-mailed and given me listings that I previously did not know about. Others have come from travel books, books about the state, websites, and personal observation.

The list may not be complete, but it is as thorough as I could make it at this time. Included are not only those towns that actually have signs alerting travelers to their claim to fame, but also others whose claims are made in other ways, but that have not been prideful enough to make note of it with a sign. Instead of simply a listing of these signs and claims to fame, I felt it would be interesting to include some information about the origins of the claims. Thus, there is a brief description of why a town claims to be the capital, birthplace, or home of something important to them, rather than just a notation of the claim. Not included are towns that have signs that are little more than advertisements, enticements, or marketing slogans that say things such as "Your Hometown Community," "Garden City, USA," "City of Adventure," etc. I felt these were too generic and didn't really represent the history or flavor of those towns.

In addition, there are some towns included that don't promote their famous citizens or important historic or cultural icons. They were included because their towns' contributions seemed significant enough to warrant inclusion. I could not include every town with a famous person, but did include some that were intertwined with those communities or of special interest.

My apologies if I missed some towns or their claims. Those may be added in future editions.

INTRODUCTION:

There are signs of pride throughout Wisconsin. A peculiar thing in the Badger state is how it seems that virtually every town makes some kind of claim of fame for itself. It is a phenomenon that can be noticed even when driving a short distance. As you near pretty much any town in the state you will encounter a billboard or some kind of sign that proclaims what it is that the town considers its connection to glory. Some of them are of national historical significance, such as Ripon's claim as the birthplace of the Republican Party. Some are of importance for the state or region, such as Belmont, the first Capital of Wisconsin. Many are amusing, confusing, or downright mysterious.

A large number of the signs proclaim the city the capital of something, such as Bloomer, the Jump Rope Capital of the World. Others realize they are not of global significance and make themselves a capital only within the boundaries of Wisconsin, such as Belleville, the U. F. O. Capital of Wisconsin. Far more don't want to take on the responsibility that comes with being the capital of anything and simply mark themselves as the birthplace or home of someone or something important.

Some Wisconsin cities and towns consider themselves to be so important that they do not stop with just one claim to fame. Green Bay is one example. Everyone in Wisconsin knows that Green Bay is called Titletown, U. S. A. because the Packers won the first two Super Bowls, but how many know it is also the Toilet Paper Capital of the World? Sauk Prairie is the place "where eagles soar," but it was also the home of prolific Wisconsin writer, August Derleth.

Other towns, not blessed with being the birthplace or home of anyone or anything of note, and not being able to make a claim as the capital of anything in particular, make do with what they have. Anyone who has ever driven near Madison has probably heard the expression, "The only Waunakee in the World." There is a sign as you enter Waunakee that marks this fact. Like all the listings in this book, it is just one of many signs of pride throughout the Badger state.

SPECIAL NOTE: Museums and other tourist sites sometimes go out of business or change hours without notice. Annual events may also cease operating or change their usual dates. Information was accurate at time of publication, but please check with the venue or organization in advance if planning a visit to any sites or events listed in this book.

A

ABBOTSFORD: Wisconsin's First City

Abbotsford's nickname is not because it is the oldest city in the state, or the richest, or the biggest, or anything else you might suspect. It is, simply, that it is the first city alphabetically in a list of Wisconsin cities and towns. Fortunately for the city, no one thought to name their city Aaron, or Triple A something the way many businesses do in order to appear first on alphabetical lists. Every August, and surprisingly not on the first weekend, the city's claim is celebrated with a weekend festival called First City Days, with events such as tractor pulls, car show, petting zoo, dancing to the Wisconsin state dance, the polka, and a Sunday morning community breakfast.

ALBANY: Pearl of the Sugar River

While this claim sounds like one of the more marketing-oriented slogans, it does acknowledge the history and local flavor of the village, which sits prettily alongside the meandering Sugar River. In the 19th century the Sugar River came to be known as the River of Pearls, as there were clams and mussels in exceptionally large numbers in the water that in some cases produced magnificent pearls. The mollusks were also found in several other southern Wisconsin rivers. Many fine pearls came from the Sugar River and a "pearl rush" began in the late 1800s that lasted about a decade. Like the California gold rush, many who came left empty-handed, but some lucky pearl hunters found pearls that made them large amounts of money. The area became a major supplier of pearls to wealthy Americans and Europeans, among others. A strand of pearls from the Sugar River can be found today at the Tower of London alongside other crown jewels. The modern-day slogan pays homage to that history.

ALGOMA: Charter Fishing Capital
              Salmon and Trout Capital of the Midwest
              Coho Capital of the Midwest
              Sport Fishing Capital of the Great Lakes

Algoma is one of those towns that won't constrain itself as the capital of one thing. Maybe they should just call themselves the Fish Capital given that all of their nicknames are related to fishing. The four titles (and who knows, possibly more) make it clear that fishing is big, big business in the area. The city, located on Lake Michigan, still maintains some commercial fishing, but most of the fishing done in the area is now sport fishing. Many visitors like to fish on the big lake, but there is also great fishing on the Ahnapee River and other inland waterways. Fishing fans enjoy their sport year-round, including ice fishing during the winter, with specific times and locations that are best for particular kinds of fish. To help them, there are at least ten charter fishing companies in operation. State record holder chinook salmon, brown trout, rainbow trout, and steelhead have all been caught in Algoma's waters. There is an annual Kewaunee/Door County Salmon Tournament at which many large salmon have been reeled in by lucky fishers and an annual Shanty Days Fishing Contest in August.

ALMA CENTER: Strawberry Capital of Wisconsin

Host of an annual strawberry festival since 1944, Alma Center bills itself as the Strawberry Capital of the state. The Strawberry Festival is put on by the Lions' Club and is held every June. A parade and other events are featured. A Strawberry Queen is crowned, and strawberry shortcakes and other treats are eaten in large quantities. It is not the only strawberry festival around the state, and not even the largest, but it is the only one located in the Strawberry Capital. Years ago, there were many strawberry patches around the area. Though there are still some strawberry growers around Alma Center, many others have disappeared over the years. Still, the town's enthusiasm for strawberries remains.

ANTIGO: Gateway to Wisconsin's Northwoods
            Origin of the Name of Wisconsin's State Soil

Located close to the center of the state, Antigo considers itself the Gateway to the Northwoods, as many tourists from other states and from southern Wisconsin pass through the area to get to the Badger state's two national forests and some of the finest state parks, many of which are deep in the forests of the northern woods. Anything north of Wausau, which is situated nearby along Highway 51, or Antigo, is considered the state's Northwoods, where many visitors get back to peace and quiet, nature and wildlife.

Most states have official state birds, state flowers, and more. Not everyone knows that more than 20 states also have their own official state soil. Wisconsin named one to remind everyone of the importance of our ecological resources. It was one of the first states to declare a state soil, and for the Badger state it is Antigo silt loam. There are more than 800 different types of soil in the state, so any one of those could have been chosen. A state historical marker on highway 52 near Antigo details the history of the soil, which is known as a productive agricultural soil. Antigo silt loam became our state soil by an act of the Legislature in 1983. A leading proponent of Antigo silt loam was University of Wisconsin soils professor, Francis Hole, who worked hard to convince the Legislature to name it. As part of his lobbying effort, he wrote "The Antigo Silt Loam Song," and also created a logo to honor the soil. Antigo and the surrounding area are where you can find the state soil, though it stretches as far away as parts of Minnesota.

APPLETON: Home of . . .

Appleton doesn't have a single claim to fame on a billboard, but it is known as the home of the following, among other things: Harry Houdini, Edna Ferber, the world's first hydroelectric generating plant, the first house with electric power, the world's first electric trolley, and the place that Joseph McCarthy considered his home.

Known as the world's greatest magician and escape artist, Harry Houdini was born in Hungary and spent part of his childhood in Appleton. His family came to the city when Houdini, born Ehrich Weisz, was only a few years old. His father was hired to serve as the first rabbi to Appleton's small Jewish community, but was later let go and the family moved to Milwaukee. As a result, Houdini only lived in Appleton for about four years. Despite that, he claimed to have been born there instead of Hungary and claimed it as his home. In return, Appleton claims him as its native son. Today, the History Museum at the Castle, formerly the Houdini Historical Center, has an exhibit on the magician where one can learn all about Houdini and his tricks and see artifacts that he used in his performances.

Though her family didn't move there until she was 12 years old, Appleton also claims Edna Ferber as its own. The Pulitzer Prize-winning writer was born in Kalamazoo, Michigan, but spent her later childhood in Appleton, where she penned her first published short story and novel. She attended college at Lawrence University in Appleton. Ferber's 1924 novel, *So Big*, won the Pulitzer Prize for fiction, making her one of the first women to ever win the prize (Edith Wharton had first done so in 1921). Other well-known novels by Ferber include *Showboat*, *Cimarron*, and *Giant*, all made into successful movies. She was also a playwright.

Appleton apparently took to electricity at an early time as the city lays claim as home of the world's first hydroelectric generating plant, as well as the first house lit by hydroelectric power. The plant started producing electricity in September of 1882. The house, Hearthstone, was lit up that same month. It is now a museum, and the original switches and chandeliers still work. Appleton also claims the world's first electric trolley, the Appleton Electric Street Railway, which began operations in 1886.

Though he was born next door in Grand Chute, Appleton has always considered Joseph McCarthy its native son. Tail Gunner Joe, as he was called due to his embellished World War II experiences, grew up in the Appleton area and became famous for his service as chair of the House Un-American Activities Committee (HUAC). In the 1950s, the committee investigated American citizens and organizations suspected of being Communist or having Communist sympathies. Not sure what it is about the Appleton area and anti-communism, but the John Birch Society was also founded in the area. See the listing for Grand Chute for more details on the John Birch Society and on McCarthy and his career.

ARGYLE: Gateway to Yellowstone
            Boyhood Home of "Fighting" Bob La Follette

No, Argyle is *not* the way to "Old Faithful" at Yellowstone National Park, and there are no geysers anywhere near it. Rather, it is the gateway to Yellowstone Lake, a 450-acre man-made lake, which is one of only a few lakes in the southwestern part of the state, and one of Wisconsin's state parks. While Fayette is much closer to

Yellowstone, Argyle is situated along the state highway from which most visitors come, and they pass through Argyle to get to the park, making it the most likely gateway to the park.

Argyle is the boyhood home of Robert "Fighting Bob" La Follette, U. S. Representative from 1885-1891, Governor of Wisconsin from 1901-1906, and U. S. Senator from 1906 until his death in 1925. He was the driving force behind the Progressive Party and ran for President as a Progressive in 1924. His is one of the two Wisconsin statues in the National Statuary Hall in the Capitol in Washington, DC. LaFollette spent eight years of his youth in the Saxton House in Argyle. The house was purchased by Historic Argyle to refurbish and turn into a local history museum. While it covers other local history, the museum's emphasis is on the life, and particularly the boyhood, of LaFollette. During the tourist season, it is open from 10:00 a.m. to 2:00 p.m. on Saturdays and by appointment.

AUGUSTA: Home of the Amish

Amish settlements are scattered throughout Wisconsin. The state has the fourth highest population of Amish in the United States. Augusta claims to be the Home of the Amish, although the settlement there is not the largest in the state. The Amish came to the Augusta area in the late 1970s, so they have been part of the local landscape for 50 years. Located in Eau Claire County, there are approximately 150 Amish families around the town. Besides having many Amish farmers in the surrounding area who may sell goods from roadside stands, one can find Amish furniture, handicrafts, and baked goods in area retail establishments. Tours of the surrounding Amish countryside that last about one and a half to two hours are available.

B

BABCOCK: Cranberry Pie Capital

Wisconsin is consistently the nation's leading producer of cranberries, which became the official state fruit in 2004. The state supplies over half of the world's cranberries every year. Located at the southwest corner of the 50-mile long Cranberry Highway, Babcock is in the heart of Wisconsin's cranberry country, a swath of land that produces most of the state's cranberries. The town has several cranberry companies, including the one most well-known, Ocean Spray. There is a café, Bucks and Berries, noted for its cranberry pies. The restaurant exports their pies to all parts of the country, as well as selling them in their own location.

BARABOO: Birthplace of the Ringling Brothers Circus
              Home of Circus World Museum
              Home of the International Clown Hall of Fame
              Home of the International Crane Foundation

The famous Ringling Brothers Circus was founded in Baraboo in 1884 and was based in the town. In 1882, five of the Ringling Brothers started a vaudeville-style show and then adapted it into a circus a couple of years after they started the show. Two other brothers joined the circus later. While regionally popular at first, the circus had a growth spurt when they switched from traveling in beautifully decorated circus wagons to the railroads. Moving the show by rail opened up the performances to any location in the country. It became one of the biggest shows in the country. Ringling Brothers eventually merged with its biggest competitor and became the Ringling Brothers and Barnum and Bailey Circus, which dominated the industry for years as The Greatest Show on Earth. Elephants were removed from the shows in 2015 and by 2017 Ringling Brothers and Barnum and Bailey closed. The current owners announced it would reopen in 2023 with no animals, but with lots of exciting entertainment for the whole family.

Over 100 circuses besides the Ringling Brothers got their starts in Wisconsin. Because of this and because of the Ringling Brothers starting their circus in Baraboo, the city is home to the Circus World Museum, located on the former site of the Ringling Brothers winter headquarters. Visitors can view live circus performances and all sorts of circus artifacts. The sprawling museum houses the world's largest collection of antique circus wagons. About 250 of them are owned by the museum. For years, many of the wagons were loaded onto flatcars and transported to Milwaukee to participate in the annual Great Circus Parade, an event that is no longer held. Residents of every town along the route from Baraboo to Milwaukee lined the tracks to catch a glimpse of the colorful antique wagons as they passed. While a big part of the collection, circus wagons are not all the museum owns. There is a large library, photographs, circus posters, and other memorabilia.

The International Clown Hall of Fame and Research Center is located just a few minutes from Circus World Museum. The Hall was founded in Delavan, another Wisconsin town noted for its circus history. It moved to downtown Milwaukee in 1997, went out of business for a while, then reopened in Baraboo. In addition to the Hall of Fame, which honors famous clowns such as Red Skelton, Emmett Kelly, Captain Kangaroo, and others, there is a small museum documenting clown history and archives containing circus posters, correspondence, and other artifacts related to the art of clowning.

The International Crane Foundation is an organization dedicated to the conservation of the world's crane population. Every species of crane in the world can be viewed at the site just a few miles outside of Baraboo and it is the only place in the world that houses all 15 species. Most of those species are endangered. Founded in 1971 by Ron Sauey and George Archibald, there are now several offices worldwide as well as the headquarters in Wisconsin. The foundation has a breeding facility where they breed cranes and then introduce the birds into the wild. Seeing these amazing birds, such as the whooping crane, can be breathtaking as that particular species is endangered with only about 700 left in the world, and that's counting those in captivity.

BARRON: Turkey Capital of Wisconsin

Barron is not the *wild* turkey capital—that is claimed elsewhere—but instead achieved fame for its turkey farms and processors. In 1941 a turkey farm was started in the city by Wallace Jerome, who later came to be known as Mr. Turkey, hopefully a name he appreciated. He helped popularize many turkey products including turkey burgers, turkey ham, turkey sausage, and more. The business was originally called Jerome Farms, and later The Turkey Store. A year after its founding, the farm had already grown to include 15,000 turkeys. By 1959, two and a half million turkeys were processed in a year. It eventually became the world's largest turkey processor. The Turkey Store became a local attraction and is now owned by Jenny-O, a division of Hormel. The Jenny-O Turkey Store is still a top attraction in the county.

BAYFIELD: Gateway to the Apostle Islands
                Berry Capital of Wisconsin
                Home of the Lake Superior Big Top Chautauqua

The Apostle Islands is a national lakeshore consisting of more than 20 gorgeous Lake Superior islands with 12 miles of coastline at the tip of northern Wisconsin. The Apostle Islands have a greater concentration of lighthouses in one place than any other coastline in America. To get there most travelers come through the gateway of Bayfield. A ferry can be taken from Bayfield to the largest and most settled of these islands, Madeline Island, where one can shop, dine, or lodge in La Pointe, visit Big Bay State Park, or enjoy some of the lighthouses. Water taxis are also available. Some people take their own boat or even kayak to the island. Once the lake is frozen over between Madeline Island and Bayfield, an ice road is created that allows cars to drive the two miles to the island atop the ice. Transportation from the mainland is also accomplished with a vehicle known as a windsled, which runs when the ice is too thick for boats to get through, but not thick enough to form the ice road that cars can take. The windsleds are propelled by large fans.

Bayfield has a long history of berry production. It is home of the largest raspberry producer in the state, but there is an incredible variety of berries that grow in the area. Blueberries, cherries, blackberries, gooseberries, juneberries, and strawberries are big, along with other fruit like apples, pears, plums, and grapes. Berries are even celebrated with a self-guided tour called the Bayfield Fruit Loop. The drive takes tourists past stores, apple orchards, wineries, and small fruit stands selling the bounty of the area. Most of the farms and orchards allow visitors to pick their own fruit, but also sell pre-packaged goods.

The Lake Superior Big Top Chautauqua is a tent show venue that showcases big-name national acts like Johnny Cash, Bonnie Raitt, and others, as well as supporting local and regional artists, presenting lectures, and premiering original music and storytelling featuring the house musicians, the Blue Canvas Orchestra and Singers. Performances are in a canvas big top tent that seats around 900 people. The house orchestra also tours. The organization produces a radio program, "Tent Show Radio," which is broadcast around the country on public radio.

BEAR CREEK: Home of the World's Largest Sauerkraut Plant

Founded by a pair of Irish brothers, Henry and Dave Flanagan, GLK Foods is now the world's leading producer of sauerkraut, popular in a state with so many citizens of German heritage. It started as a pickling company in 1900 and handled a small amount of cabbage at first. The company has worked with some cabbage farms year after year for a hundred years or more and processes up to 150,000 tons of sauerkraut a year. The great-grandson of Dave Flanagan is now the owner of the business. St. Mary's parish hosts an annual sauerkraut festival to celebrate the product that is so important to the local economy. It features games, a dinner, and food items such as sauerkraut hot dish and sauerkraut cupcakes. There is also a Bear Creek Kraut run featuring 5k and 10k races, as well as children's runs.

BELGIUM: The Village with a Heart

While it sounds like a warm and fuzzy ad campaign, there are green hearts, not red, on the welcome sign, and there is some history behind the reason for it. Belgium, Wisconsin was founded by settlers from Luxembourg (the part that was at the time annexed and ruled by Belgium) in the mid-19th century. The village of Belgium still retains pride in its roots. Luxembourg is known as the Green Heart of Europe. Thus, the hearts on the village sign recognize the village's Luxembourg heritage, while the name recognizes the country ruling their home territory at the time the first settlers came to Wisconsin. The town is home to the Luxembourg American Cultural Society, which provides education about Luxembourg and its immigrants through programs and a museum. The village has held a Luxembourg Festival since 1987, which features games and food, including a treipen (or träipen) eating contest. Treipen is the Luxembourgian version of black pudding or blood sausage. At the 2022 celebration a sculpture called "Immigration," by immigrant artist Victorine Hinger was unveiled at the village square during the festival.

BELLEVILLE: UFO Capital of Wisconsin

The city is alternately described as the UFO Capital of Wisconsin or occasionally of the World. Belleville takes full advantage of its nickname by hosting numerous UFO activities around Halloween every year. This includes activities ranging from a parade to a Monster's Ball to a haunted trail. It started in 1987 when a police officer initially saw a cluster of lights in the sky. He and several other police officers later reported seeing a UFO, a non-moving object with flashing lights about 1,000 feet up in the air. Eventually the lights moved away and disappeared. Over the next several months citizens filed over 40 similar reports. National media reported on the story and UFO investigators descended on the town to determine whether the sightings were real. They decided that what the residents had seen were genuine UFO sightings. After the spring of that year the sightings and reports stopped. By then the citizens were calling the city the UFO capital and it stuck. For competitors to this title see the listings for Dundee and Elmwood.

BELMONT: First Capitol of Wisconsin

Back in the 1820s and 1830s, when Wisconsin was still a territory, the southwestern part of the state was the most populated due to an influx of lead miners from all over the world. As a result, the first meeting of the Territorial Legislature was held at Belmont in the winter of 1836. The legislators met for more than 40 days and enacted about an equal number of laws in their first session. Included was a decision to make Madison the permanent capital of the state, though it didn't even exist as a city at the time. Political maneuvering by Judge James Doty, who owned much of the land in what became Madison, led to the adoption of the area as the permanent state capital. At the time, the entirety of the current states of Wisconsin, Iowa, and Minnesota, as well as parts of the Dakotas, were included in the Wisconsin Territory. The second legislative meeting was held in what is now Burlington, Iowa, so the second capital city of the Wisconsin Territory was in a city in present-day Iowa. Eventually

Madison became the seat of government and remains so to this day. Both the Council House and the Supreme Court building were removed for several years from the Belmont site and were used as houses. The Council House was also used as a livestock barn for some time. Thanks to the efforts of the Wisconsin Federation of Women's Clubs, it was moved back to its original site in 1924 and restored. The Supreme Court building was moved back in 1956. Two other buildings from the original site, a lodging house for legislators and a residence for the governor, no longer exist. Today, the original Legislature and Supreme Court buildings can be visited at a small park near Belmont Mound, just a few miles outside the town of Belmont. It is operated by the Wisconsin Historical Society and is free.

BELOIT: Gateway to Wisconsin
Home of America's First Angel Museum
Home of the World's Largest Chili Can

Beloit bills itself as the Gateway to Wisconsin due to the fact that it straddles the Illinois border. In fact, South Beloit is across the border in Illinois. There are other towns that lie on the border between the two states, but most of them are small towns, except for Racine and Kenosha in the southeastern part of the state. There is likely more traffic that crosses from Illinois into Beloit than any other border town in the south-central part of the state.

While it was never an official city title, Beloit was home of the world's largest angel museum. It also claimed to be the first. Due to lack of funds (or donations from angelic benefactors) it closed in 2018 and the collections were auctioned off. There were two separate collections, the Berg Collection, which consisted of thousands of angels, and the Black Angel Collection, which consisted of over 600 African American angels sent to television host Oprah Winfrey by her fans, and subsequently donated by Winfrey to the museum. The two primary collections and more combined to give visitors over 11,000 angel artifacts to view, including over 6,000 angels. Of course, there was also a gift shop and a restaurant, appropriately named the Taste of Heaven Cafe. The museum made a point of noting that it did not intend to promote any particular theological point of view.

Finally, and a little wackier than the other two claims, Beloit is home of the World's Largest Chili Can. The gigantic cylinder is located at the local Hormel plant and is a nearly 2,000-gallon storage tank painted like a can of Hormel Chili (with Beans). For perspective, only the top half of the tank is painted; otherwise, the can would be too elongated and not look like the real product. It is on the company's private property, but is visible from the Interstate highway.

BENTON: Mining Capital of Wisconsin
             Home of Father Samuel Mazzuchelli

No longer a mining community--all the mines have closed--Benton was founded by lead miners who came to southwestern Wisconsin in the early part of the 19th century. The hundreds of mines in that part of the state produced tremendous amounts of lead and zinc when they were operating. The last of the mines in the area closed in the late 1960s and early 1970s. The economy now centers around farming, but citizens still take great pride in their mining heritage. On Main Street visitors can find Swindler's Ridge Museum which features local history and mining artifacts from the days when the town was inhabited almost entirely by miners. It is only open from Friday through Monday during the tourist season.

The last parish served by frontier missionary priest, Samuel Mazzuchelli, was Benton's St. Patrick's parish, which he founded and where he served for about 12 years. It was said the Irish miners in the area called their beloved Italian priest Father Matthew Kelly. Mazzuchelli founded many of the early Catholic parishes and schools in Wisconsin, Iowa, and Illinois and designed and built about two dozen churches and civic buildings, including St. Patrick's and many others in the surrounding area. In addition to the churches and other civic buildings he was responsible for, he also founded the order of Dominican Sisters at nearby Sinsinawa, Wisconsin. Residents of the area have pushed for years to have him canonized as a saint and in 1993 he was declared "venerable" by Pope John Paul II, one of the steps leading toward possible sainthood. He died at Benton in 1864 and is buried in a small cemetery behind the church.

BERLIN: Fur and Leather Capital of the World
             Home of the First Commercial Cranberry Operations

in Wisconsin

Originally, Berlin's fur and leather trade literally developed as a fur and leather *trade*, as early trappers engaged in bartering with the local Native American population and traded goods for pelts. Situated along the Fox River, which was used by early French fur traders, it was a natural location to develop businesses to turn fur and hides into products such as fur coats, moccasins, fine gloves, and more. As time went on, fur and leather factories were built in the town and it soon laid claim as the world capital of both industries. Sometimes with the passage of time a town's claim to fame changes or disappears entirely. The Berlin Area Historical Society's website notes that "from the mid 1860's to the late 1990's Berlin was known as the 'fur and leather city' because of the multiple businesses" located there and even the city website says, "once the fur and leather capital," indicating that despite the history they don't claim it anymore.

The city does lay claim the home of the first commercial cranberry operations in the state. Cranberries were first harvested in Wisconsin by Edward Sacket in Berlin in the mid-1800s. He was producing hundreds of barrels of cranberries by the mid-1860s and soon others followed suit. Now there are between 200 and 250 cranberry growers in the state, which leads the nation in cranberry production.

BIRCHWOOD: Bluegill Capital of Wisconsin

While occasionally called the Bluegill Capital of the World, a 14-foot-long fiberglass bluegill on a pole as tourists enter town proclaims Birchwood as the Bluegill Capital of Wisconsin. Given how important the sport of fishing is in the state any claim to fame that rests on being the capital of any type of fish is sure to gain attention. Unlike some cities that battle over other fish species, Birchwood has no competition in the realm of bluegills. There are multiple lakes in the immediate area, including Lake Chetac and Long Lake. In all of them are numerous fish species besides the famed bluegills, including walleye, pike, bass, and more. Like any good capital there is a festival associated with the town's claim to fame. The annual Bluegill Festival is always held the third weekend of July, featuring music, games, a fish fry, a Miss Bluegill crowning, and a bluegill fishing contest. Not to leave winter feeling left out there is also a Birchwood Bluegill Christmas Fest, held annually on the first Saturday of December.

BIRNAMWOOD: Home of the World's Largest Badger
                         Home pf the World's Largest Squirrel

The world's largest badger is a huge monster with frightening claws that rises from the ground in front of a former gas station that is now a gentlemen's club. The giant badger greets (or scares) visitors to Birnamwood. The badger state's best-known symbol reduced to greeting visitors at a strip club seems like a travesty, but it is what it is. The site used to be a well-known tourist stop where travelers pulled in to gas up their car and replenish supplies for the road. Now most traveling families speed by and don't stop. The location is also home of the world's largest fiberglass squirrel, which lives behind the badger on the property, standing atop a giant log. To paraphrase a Tennessee Williams title, it's something of a fiberglass menagerie. At one time the badger was 40 feet tall and loomed over visitors from the rooftop of the gas station, but most of its body has been removed, so it is significantly shorter now. The squirrel scampers across a log that is big enough to drive a car through. In fact, it is now used as a garage, and was once where cars pulled through to reach the gas pumps.

BLACK CREEK: Birthplace of the First Organized National Baseball Team

Founded by L. J. Cook, the Black Creek baseball team was formed in 1869 and is said to be the First Organized National Baseball Team in the country. The Cincinnati Reds, originally the Red Stockings, are considered to be the first *professional* baseball team and also got their start in 1869. It's always been a curiosity how the first team of a sport could form if there were no other teams to play, but it has to start somewhere. Cook's team mostly played against teams that formed in other small towns in the area and lasted into the 1990s when it was disbanded. An annual "grudge match" softball game is held every year to honor the history of baseball in the town, a seemingly odd choice for the commemoration.

BLACK RIVER FALLS: Deer Capital of Wisconsin

Just off the highway, at Black River Crossing, one can view a large orange moose, a mouse investigating a piece of cheese, and a fiberglass deer leaping over a log, the last one appropriate for the Deer Capital of Wisconsin. Both Jackson County and the county seat, Black River Falls, lay claim to Deer Capital of Wisconsin. Black River Falls is located close to the Jackson County Forest and the Black River State Forest, which both help to make the area a big hunting destination, especially when deer season rolls around. There are 200,000 acres of public land for hunters and nature lovers to explore, with plenty of Wisconsin's state wildlife animal to be found. With deer hunting season being celebrated with an almost religious fervor in the state, claiming to be the Deer Capital is smart for the local economy and backed up by a good-sized population of white-tails.

BLOOMER: Jump Rope Capital of the World

The annual World Jump Roping Contest is a speed jump rope contest held in Bloomer every year on the last Saturday in January. Originally introduced in 1960 by physical education teacher Wally Mohrman as a way to further his students' interest in rope jumping as a physical activity the contest grew over the years, earning Bloomer the title of Jump Rope Capital of the World.. Now about 250 young people a year vie for the top prize by jumping 60 to 70 or more times in just ten seconds. There is also an adult division. Trophies are given out annually for the best speed jump ropers from all the competing schools in each of the divisions. Wally Mohrman and record holder Paul Morning appeared on "The Tonight Show" with Johnny Carson in 1980 and gained national TV exposure for the city and for rope jumping. Mohrman also appeared on the show "Real People" a couple of years later. Decades later, Morning's record of 72 jumps in ten seconds is still unbroken.

BONDUEL: Spelling Capital of Wisconsin
              Home of the Bears

After a string of state spelling bee champions hailed from Bonduel in the 1980s the city declared itself the Spelling Capital of Wisconsin, and they even used the correct spelling of capital. The title was well-earned. The school's math teacher, Myles Belke, served as the coach for the school's spelling bee. In a seven-year span, five of the state's spelling bee champions were from Bonduel.

The village is called Home of the Bears due to a local legend about the Jesuit missionary, Florimond Bonduel, after whom the town was named. The priest served Catholics around the area and helped the Menominee people settle on their reservation in the mid-1800s. He worked to convert members of the tribe and was the first to translate the Lord's Prayer into Menominee. He was said to have been attacked by an assailant, but two bears came to his rescue and saved him from his attacker. Supposedly, the bears followed him after that and served as his protectors. The school's nickname is the Bonduel Bears.

BOSCOBEL: Birthplace of the Gideon Bible
                     Wisconsin's Turkey Hunting Capital

This is not a traveling salesman joke. One day in 1898 a traveling salesman walked into a hotel. He tried to check into the Boscobel Hotel, originally called Central House. There were no rooms left, so the manager asked if the visitor would mind sharing a room with another man. Being a good Christian man he may have hesitated, but needing a place to sleep, he agreed. It turned out his roommate for the night was also a good Christian traveling salesman and after some discussion the two hatched a plan to form a Christian travelers' association. This association became the Gideon Society, which more than 100 years later is the organization responsible for placing millions upon millions of Gideon Bibles in hotels, motels, and inns all over the world.

There are apparently many turkeys around the Boscobel area, as it billed itself for years as Wisconsin's Turkey Hunting Capital. A large fiberglass turkey welcomes visitors to the town, and there is a wooden sign noting the town's capital status. Several years ago, it was thought the title was too limiting given all of the activities available in the area, so a marketing team decided to rebrand Boscobel as Wisconsin's Outdoor Recreation Destination, which most Wisconsin communities could claim based on the natural beauty of the state. Sometimes marketing teams miss the obvious and unique features of what they are trying to sell. Despite the rebranding, at last report the fiberglass turkey still welcomes all to the town.

BOULDER JUNCTION: Musky Capital of the World
                    Home of the Great White Wonder

The muskellunge (musky for short) is Wisconsin's official state fish. Boulder Junction is the home of an unusually high number of freshwater lakes--there are almost 300 lakes within ten miles of the city--including more than 50 class A musky lakes. It is said that more muskies are caught in this area than anywhere else. To draw attention to this, there is an 18-foot-long fiberglass musky named Marty the Musky in front of the local Chamber of Commerce. The city hosts an annual musky tournament, the World Championship Musky Classic, which occurs in the fall. In the summer, it is home to the annual Musky Jamboree, featuring fishing workshops and competitions, live music, an antique auto show, and an arts and craft fair. There was a long-running debate with Hayward, however, about which city could lay claim as the Musky Capital of the World. Boulder Junction had registered the title with the state in 1950 and ultimately prevailed when it received a trademark from the federal government's Patent and Trademark Office in 1971. These days, apparently to avoid infringing on the official trademark, Hayward bills itself as the Muskie Capital of the World, proving that spelling can be important in life.

Boulder Junction and the surrounding area are known for a large herd of white deer, sometimes called ghost deer because of their appearance. Seeing one of these in the wild is an incredible experience. They are pure white with pink noses and ears. The deer are true albinos and while albino deer are generally rare, for some reason there are large numbers of them around Boulder Junction. There is no scientific explanation for the concentration of them in such a limited area. The herd is one of the highlights of the community featured on the Travel Boulder Junction website.

BOYCEVILLE: Cucumber Capital of Wisconsin

For many years, a pickle company called Gedney's was a large employer in the town of Boyceville. There were many cucumber fields in the area and local growers could get good money from Gedney's for their cucumbers. Every year for decades the town has celebrated cucumbers with a Cucumber Festival, sometimes called the Pickle Festival, even though the company left town many years ago. The festival occurs in August and is the big social event of the year for residents and visitors alike. Highlights over the years have included a parade, a cucumber carving festival, pickle eating contest, tractor pull, the Cucumber Run, and the crowning of the Cucumber Queen.

BRODHEAD: Home of the Clarence Covered Bridge

Long after most of the covered bridges in Wisconsin were torn down, the citizens of Brodhead longed for the good old days when they had one. The original, which spanned the Sugar River, was destroyed in 1931 when a truck crashed through its floor. In 1984, cooperation between the citizens of the community, the Department of Natural Resources, and the local chapter of the Jaycees led to the rebuilding of the Clarence Covered Bridge. A replica of the original bridge now spans Norwegian Creek and was built along the Sugar River Bicycle Trail. It is used by scores of bikers and hikers who travel on the trail. Like other towns that celebrate their unique claim to fame, Brodhead hosts a three-day celebration called Covered Bridge Days every August. It is combined with a celebration of wildflowers, with wildflower walks and an annual wildflower art display.

BRUSSELS: Home of America's Largest Belgian Settlement

The international city of Brussels is the capital of Belgium and was chosen as the name of the Door County town to honor its first settlers, a group of four immigrant families from Belgium who originally founded the town. Others soon followed. The Belgian settlement in Wisconsin extended across three counties and a part of it called the Namur District was the first rural community in the country named as a National Historic Landmark. Two other towns in the area have a higher percentage of Belgian-Americans than Brussels and the top five in the country are all in the area, making it America's Largest Belgian Settlement. Brussels is the home of the Belgian Heritage Center, which works to preserve the history, Walloon language, and culture of the Belgian immigrants to the area. Small votive chapels built by Belgian settlers are scattered around the district The Belgian heritage is honored with the annual Belgian Kermis Festival in September. Kermis is a fair or festival that is primarily held to raise funds for a charity, in this case the Lions Club. Belgian waffles, trippe (a Belgian sausage with sauerkraut inside), booyah (a thick Belgian stew), jutt (a Belgian fried cabbage dish), and Belgian pies are served. Brussels was one of the towns destroyed in the Peshtigo fire of 1871, and while many communities simply disappeared after the fire, Brussels was one of the towns rebuilt by its citizens.

BURLINGTON: Chocolate City, U. S. A.
Home of the Liars' Club
Home of the Spinning Top and Yo-Yo Museum

How can you top a city with three such diverse claims to fame? Burlington hosts almost two dozen annual events. The big one was always the annual ChocolateFest, held over a weekend every year in May for more than 30 years. It was a chocolate lover's delight. The Chocolate City name arose because Burlington is home to a Nestlé chocolate and confections factory. While the factory is still open and employs many citizens of the city, it no longer offers tours of the facility, which used to be a tourist draw. Elsewhere in town visitors can still tour the Chocolate Experience Museum with displays of chocolate carvings, and there are still a couple of confectioners in the city that sell chocolate and other sweet treats. However, the city is moving away from its Chocolate City U. S. A. brand and searching for a new identity with the help of some marketing experts. Much to the chagrin of Wisconsin chocolate lovers, ChoclateFest was replaced in 2021 with a jamboree due to the rebranding effort and the Covid pandemic, as well as less participation from vendors. The money raised from the former festival was always recycled back into the community and the same non-profit organization is running the new jamboree.

Burlington is internationally known as the Home of the Burlington Liars' Club, an organization devoted to tall tales and stories that stretch the truth maybe just a wee little bit. The organization was founded in 1929 by friends who appropriately enough made up a news story about their liars' club, which didn't exist prior to that time. The story took off and was carried by newspapers around the country, leading to the men deciding they needed to create the Burlington Liars Club, which to this day sponsors an annual contest to find the best exaggerated story. The winner gets a trophy and the notoriety that comes with being a champion liar. The city has even devised a walking tour, the Tall Tales Trail, which highlights many of the historic buildings in the town.

Finally, no visit to Burlington would be complete without a visit to the Spinning Top and Yo-Yo Museum, which features close to 2,000 tops, yo-yos, and similar toys housed in a small storefront downtown. The museum tour is guided and includes interactive activity with 40 hands-on tops and games to play, demonstrations, videos, and more. Tours are at specific times. They also offer classes and workshops. The toy shop was open, but the museum closed, during the pandemic. Please check in advance to verify whether the museum has reopened.

BYRON: Birthplace of Steve Wittman

In the world of experimental aircraft and air racing, Steve Wittman was known to everyone. A member of the Wisconsin Aviation Hall of Fame, Motorsports Hall of Fame of America, and the National Aviation Hall of Fame, he won many air races and designed some of the most popular race planes during his air-racing career. He was also a test pilot. For almost 40 years he ran the Oshkosh Municipal Airport, which was renamed in his honor upon his retirement. Steve and his second wife, Paula, tragically died in a plane crash in Alabama in 1995. One of his planes, Buster, can be viewed today at the National Air and Space Museum. Several more of his airplanes are on display at the Experimental Aircraft Association (EAA) museum in Oshkosh. He was an early member of the EAA and was involved in developing the hugely popular EAA Fly-in, where experimental aircraft fly in from all over the country and beyond. Wittman was born on the second floor of the Soo Line Railroad Depot in Byron in 1904 and spent most of his childhood in the area. Despite losing most of the vision in one of his eyes as a child he became a licensed pilot in 1924. His certificate was signed by one of the Wright Brothers (some sources say it was Orville and others claim it was Wilbur). Byron has erected two signs honoring Wittman as a native son.

C

CABLE: Home of the American Birkebeiner
                    Mountain Biking Capital of the Midwest

Located in Chequamegon National Forest, Cable is home to beautiful forests and some incredible outdoor sporting events. The American Birkebeiner (Birkie, for short) is North America's largest cross country ski race. It was founded by Tony Wise, who patterned it after a similar marathon in Norway, which in turn honored two soldiers who skied 18-month-old Prince Haakon, heir to the throne, to safety during the Norwegian civil war in the early 1200s. The American event, held every February since 1973, started with 35 skiers and now draws thousands of skiers from all over the world to Cable and northern Wisconsin to compete in the 55-kilometer annual race. It draws thousands more spectators to the area. The race starts at Cable and ends on Main Street in Hayward. In addition to the main event, there are many other events held in conjunction with the Birkie, including shorter races, snowshoe hikes, and more. A fat bike Birkie is held in March.

Another race that starts and ends in the same two locations is the Chequamegon 40, one of the many Fat Tire Festival races around the country, annual events that celebrate mountain biking. The Chequamegon 40 is a 40-mile race that uses the Birkie trail, forest roads, and snowmobile trails. It is held in September. The Cable-Area Off-Road Classic is a 20-mile course and a grueling 25-mile course. The Epic Bike Fest starts in Hayward and ends in Cable. Mountain biking doesn't have to be competitive despite all the races in the area. Adding to the town's claim as the Mountain Biking Capital, there are several hundred miles of mountain biking trails in the nearby forest, available to both beginners and experienced bikers, with Cable at the center of it all.

CADOTT: Half-Way Between the Equator and the North Pole

Technically, Cadott is not the halfway point between the equator and north pole. It sits close to the 45th parallel, but that spot is really a few miles north of the town. Still, it's close enough to claim it. There is a large billboard put up by the local Lions Club proclaiming the distinction. Give the Lions credit for honesty, though. The billboard notes that the actual location is three miles north. It's in a bit smaller print, but it's there and is a testament to truth in advertising. The club originally put up a sign in 1955 at the suggestion of a resident who was into geography and felt the city should capitalize on its location. The old sign was replaced in 1999 as it was getting worn-looking. The signs had the same wording, but different background colors and the original had an arrow pointing to Cadott that was removed from the new one.

CALUMET COUNTY: Supper Club Capital of the Midwest

With more than 30 supper clubs spread around the county, Calumet County claims to have more supper clubs than any other county in Wisconsin, a state known for its supper clubs. For those non-Wisconsinites, a supper club is a restaurant that is typically only open in the evening for supper. It features homemade food, often of the meat and potato variety, as well as fish, particularly on Fridays. Even though it has the word "club" in it, it is not a club and one does not need to be a member to dine in one. Supper clubs tend to be a little more upscale looking (though some are very kitschy), but remain within the reach of the pocketbooks of their mostly rural customers. Service is slow, as the food is made to order, and patrons do not rush to eat and leave. They are sit-down places where families and friends go for a great home-cooked meal, good conversation, drinks, especially beer or brandy old-fashioneds, and a full and fun night out. Quite often, neighbors and other friends or relatives will be at the place at the same time for a night out.

CAMBRIDGE: Umbrella City

The Umbrella City name for Cambridge goes back almost a century. Back in 1938 a local merchant, Arthur Meister, promoted the idea of Cambridge as "the umbrella vacation spot," using the beach umbrellas that vacationers settle under on the beach at Lake Ripley to promote the town as a destination. The idea took hold and the town became known as Umbrella City. Umbrellas were placed on top of light poles downtown (perhaps also a novel way to reduce light pollution). Postcards and tourism materials were created highlighting the downtown umbrellas. And, of course, a festival—Umbrella Daze—was created to go along with the tourism promotion and to give the townspeople something other than the beach to look forward to every summer. While the name has mostly fallen out of use, there are still remnants in business names and imagery and for those who go to the beach, umbrellas are still available to rent.

CASHTON: Home of the Largest Amish Community in Wisconsin

In many parts of the state there are more and more Amish settlers moving in and working farms. Wisconsin now has the fourth-largest Amish population in the country. The Amish first came to Cashton in the mid-1960s and have grown to about 2,000 residents in the area. It has become one of the largest Amish settlements in the nation. The Amish are a Christian sect that for the most part live apart from society and shun technology such as cellphones and vehicles. There are more Amish in the western part of the state than anywhere else in Wisconsin. You can see their farms, horses and buggies, and the like from Tomah to Belmont, but there is a far greater likelihood of coming across Amish farms and families around the Cashton area than anywhere else in the state. There are businesses that conduct tours of the Amish farms and the local visitors' brochures ask tourists to respect the Amish people by putting cameras away as they do not want their pictures taken. Photos of buggies and farms are acceptable. Visitors are requested to honor their Sabbath, which is on Sunday as they do not wish to conduct any business on Sundays. Around the area there are many Amish farms that on Monday through Saturday will gladly sell homemade treats, quilts, furniture, candles, and more.

CATARACT: Home of the Wegner Grotto

Inspired by a grotto in Dickeyville, Wisconsin Paul and Matilda Wegner decided to build one of their own. Untrained in art, they nevertheless pushed ahead and built a small chapel and a number of sculptures on their property. Like the Dickeyville Grotto, they used concrete, broken glass, seashells, arrowheads, and other found materials to build the chapel, a large replica of their wedding cake, a sculpture of the SS Bremen, and more. Like the grotto that inspired them, many of the sculptures are religious or patriotic. Locals refer to the site as the Glass Church. The grotto is open to the public during the tourism season.

CEDARBURG: Home of the Last Covered Bridge in Wisconsin

There were once 40 or more covered bridges throughout Wisconsin. Originally called the Red Bridge, the Cedarburg Covered Bridge is the last of the original covered bridges in the state. It was built in 1876 and spans Cedar Creek in Covered Bridge County Park. All others that can be seen now in Wisconsin are replicas of the originals or new. The Cedarburg bridge is a lattice truss bridge made of pine, oak, and cedar and is 120 feet long and 12 feet wide. Its construction used wooden pegs instead of nails. In 1962 the bridge was moved about 50 feet and was replaced for vehicular traffic with a safer modern bridge. The original still stands and is available for use only by pedestrians and bicyclists. It was listed on the National Register of Historic Places in 1973.

CLAM LAKE: Elk Capital of Wisconsin

Once plentiful in Wisconsin, elk disappeared in the state in the late 1800s due to overhunting and loss of habitat. In 1995, elk were reintroduced in the state with the release of 25 elk from Michigan in the Chequamegon-Nicolet National Forest around Clam Lake. The elk range is over 1,200 square miles touching parts of five counties and is centered at Clam Lake. The original herd of 25 has grown to several hundred animals. The eventual goal is for a herd of about 1,400 animals. Additional elk from Kentucky were released at different times around Black River Falls and other areas in the northern part of the state, but the oldest, largest, and most successful herd is the one around Clam Lake. Though sightings are not guaranteed, several wildlife viewing areas have been established, which improve the chances of visitors seeing an elk in the wild. An interactive touch screen located at the Clam Lake Community Park provides updated information on the herd. And, of course, there is a fall Elk Festival. As part of the festival, there is an elk walking tour and the Department of Natural Resources provides educational outreach.

COBB: Home of the Cobb Corn Roast Festival

Home of the Cobb Corn Roast Festival is not on the town's welcome sign, but there are several cobs of corn painted onto it. There is, however, an annual corn roast held every year in August and the welcome sign does announce the date of the festival each year. Like most small-town festivals it features things like baseball, live music, rides and games, and food—in this case, a chicken barbeque. And corn. Corn on the Cobb. Sweet Corn on the Cobb. The weekend's activities end with a parade. Proceeds from the festival are funneled back into the community to help support community organizations and civic projects.

COLBY: Birthplace of Colby Cheese

There are not that many place names in the world that have been given to foods that derived there, but Colby is one of them. Developed in 1885 by Joseph Steinwand at his father's cheese factory a mile or so out of town, world-famous Colby cheese originated in the Wisconsin town and is the only natural cheese created in America. There is a state historical marker on 1st Street describing the development of the cheese. Colby cheese is often compared to a mild cheddar. The manufacturing process is similar, but departs in a few significant ways: washing the curds with cold water to stop the acidification process, pressing the curds, and aging the cheese for a much shorter time, anywhere from one to three months. Cheddar is generally aged for two to three months, up to a year or longer. The result is a milder and sweeter cheese than cheddar. The history of Colby cheese is honored with Colby Cheese Days, featuring games, a carnival, and a cheese toss. There might also be cheese to eat. Well, no "might." There will be plenty of cheese. Ironically, Colby cheese is no longer made in Colby. A large cheese factory that was built on the site where Colby cheese was developed is no longer in business. The purely Wisconsin cheese is produced at other cheese factories throughout America's Dairyland, but no longer in Colby. Cheese is Wisconsin's official state dairy product, and there has also been a push to name Colby the official state cheese.

COLGATE: Home of Paul Bobrowitz Spectacular Sculpture

Wisconsin has a good number of sculpture parks created by men with a vision who spend years creating unique and sometimes odd pieces of art out of found metal and more. Most of these sculptors are untrained folk artists with an unrelenting drive to create. Like many of them, Paul Bobrowitz has created a large number of sculptures over the course of a couple of decades by using scrap metal and found pieces to mold them (or, in this case, to weld them) into something new and unexpected. Bobrowitz has created more than a thousand pieces. Some of them have found their way into collections and exhibitions, and according to several online sites he has won several awards for his metal sculptures. His sculpture park is six acres filled with interesting creations and is free to the public. Unlike most of the folk art sites in the state, all of the pieces are available to purchase.

COLUMBUS: Redbud City

Redbud trees are beautiful trees that flower in the early spring. The flowers are a gorgeous pink to purple color and are very fragrant. The citizens of Columbus are proud of the numerous redbuds found in the city, especially along Dickason Boulevard and in yards all over own. Every May, Redbud Day is celebrated and the highlight is a Chamber of Commerce drawing in which trees are given away to citizens to grow in their yards. A new Redbud Prince and Princess are selected and there is plenty of food and music. While not native to Wisconsin, the trees have been planted by residents for years and many of them have stories to tell about their tree growing successes and failures.

COON VALLEY: Home of the Nation's First Watershed Project

The nation's first-ever water and soil conservation district was set aside near Coon Valley all the way back in 1933. The federal government, through the agency then known as the Soil Erosion Service, worked together with the University of Wisconsin to plan improvements in habitat preservation, crop rotation, terracing, and other now-common methods of preventing soil erosion. The Coon Creek Watershed covers approximately 90,000 acres across three Wisconsin counties, most of it in Vernon County. The plan helped the land become more productive, increased income for area farmers, and ultimately improved water quality. According to the historical marker about the watershed in Coon Valley, "Planned practices in effect include improvement of woodlands, wildlife habitat and pastures, better rotations and fertilization, strip cropping, terracing, and gully and stream bank erosion control." It became a model for the nation.

CORNELL: Stacker City

What, you may ask, is a stacker and why would a town call itself Stacker City? In Cornell, it is a central part of the city's history and identity and is sometimes called the Eiffel Tower of the North. Coming into the city from several highways, travelers see a 175-foot-tall pulpwood stacker standing at a 45-degree angle, leaving the possibility that it could also be nicknamed the Leaning Tower of the North. The Leaning Tower's height is considerably closer to the stacker than the Eiffel Tower, too. In its heyday the machine replaced a number of workers and stacked logs into piles that could be floated to a nearby paper mill. The stacker was used for about 60 years in the 20th century. By the early 1970s the stacker was obsolete and fell into disuse. It is located at Cornell Millyard Park and is believed to be the last remaining pulpwood stacker in the United States, if not the world. A number of other buildings on the site were destroyed by fire in 1989, but the stacker survived the blaze. It is listed on the National Register of Historic Places.

CUBA CITY: City of Presidents

There have been no United States Presidents born in Wisconsin and while several have visited the state, only one—George W. Bush in 2004—has ever made a stop in Cuba City. He gave a campaign speech at the high school nearly 30 years after the City of Presidents nickname was claimed by the city, and he even mentioned the town's nickname in his speech. So why the City of Presidents? Back in 1976, cities and individual citizens across the country were coming up with ideas to celebrate the nation's bicentennial. In Cuba City red, white, and blue shields with silhouettes of each of the Presidents, their home states, years in office, and numerical order were placed on streetlights along Main Street. The original plywood shields were replaced several times, most recently in 2014, and are now a more durable plastic. Almost 50 years after the shields were first put up for the bicentennial, the Presidents are still there, and each new President has been added as they have taken office. One of the shields has three silhouettes on it and welcomes travelers to the City of Presidents. In addition to the Presidential shields there is now a refurbished "Presidential Caboose" featuring local and Presidential history, including George W. Bush's original plywood sign which he signed during his visit. It is located on the city's Presidential Plaza along Main Street.

CUMBERLAND: Rutabaga Capital of the World

Cumberland doesn't really promote itself as the Rutabaga Capital of the World anymore, but it does hold an annual festival that honors its historic reputation as a great location for growing the rutabaga, a type of turnip. The vegetable has been successfully grown around the Cumberland area for years. The town's website has a link to further information on rutabagas, which grow well in northwestern Wisconsin due to the soil and its cooler climate. Rutabagas were shipped around the country from the area. The peak of the rutabaga trade around Cumberland was in the 1960s, and it tailed off in the following years. For the annual event there is, of course, a Rutabaga Queen and a Rutabaga run/walk event, as well as a parade, live bands, and plenty of rutabaga to eat.

$\mathcal{D}$

DELAVAN: 19th Century Circus Capital of the Nation
Clown Town, U. S. A.

Like Baraboo, there is an incredible amount of circus history in
Delavan. It started in 1847 when the Mabie brothers, Edmund and
Jeremiah, passed through Delavan with their U. S. Olympic Circus
and liked it so much they decided to buy land and winter in the city.
At the time theirs was the largest circus in the country and that drew
other circuses to come to the area as well. Eventually, many circuses
quartered in Delavan and their animals could be seen downtown
throughout much of the second half of the 19th century. The P. T.
Barnum circus was founded in Delavan and changed circus mobility
and history by moving the show by rail instead of by wagons. While
Barnum loaned his name, historians believe it was really founded by
William Coup, who convinced Barnum to start the circus and who
suggested moving it by rail. It was also his idea to add a second and a
third ring. It later merged with the Ringling Brothers and became
"the Greatest Show on Earth." In the late 1800s more than two
dozen circuses made Delavan their winter home. The city retained its
circus atmosphere until about the turn of the century, when the last
of the circuses pulled up stakes and left town. Because of its history
the town hosted the first day of issue ceremony for the U. S. Post
Office's release of a 1966 stamp honoring the circus in America.

The Post Office's circus stamp featured a clown as its central
design, a type of performer that played prominently in the latter part
of the 20th century in Delavan's history. In 1987 the International
Clown Hall of Fame was founded in the city and stayed for almost a
decade, until it moved to a home in the Grand Avenue Mall in
downtown Milwaukee. It is now located in Baraboo. Today, in a
downtown Delavan park, there is a giant fiberglass elephant with a
clown standing in front of it and a large giraffe on the opposite end
of the park. Aside from the tombstones of the dozens upon dozens
of circus performers buried in the city, the fiberglass figures and a
historical marker about the Greatest Show on Earth are the only
major reminders left of the city's circus and clown heritage. A second
historical marker on the Circus Colony is missing. It disappeared just
as the circus itself had done years before.

DICKEYVILLE: Home of the Grotto

It seems almost in humility that Dickeyville bills itself simply as the Home of the Grotto when the Grotto itself has a far less unassuming name and a gaudy appearance. It is officially known as the Grotto of Christ the King and Mary His Mother. More commonly referred to by locals simply as the Grotto, the shrine is an incredible display of religious and patriotic iconography. It was created between 1925 and 1930 by a priest, Father Matthias Wernerus, with construction assistance from his parishioners. Wernerus served as pastor of the church for 13 years and died only a year after the dedication of the shrine he built. A couple of the shrines in the garden, the Stations of the Cross and Our Lady of Fatima, were added several years after completion of the original design. The site, located on the grounds of Holy Ghost Parish, is both odd and beautiful. Heavily symbolic Christian themes are displayed alongside U. S. flags and American heroes, all built with rock, glass, gems, shells, wood, and other materials. It has a definite lack of separation of church and state. Some say it was a reflection of the priest's love of both God and country. Others believe it was designed to show Protestants that Catholics are patriotic, as many in the 1920s and 1930s believed that Catholic citizens' fealty was to the Pope, not to the United States. Either way, it's an incredible work of folk art. The Grotto is free, but donations are accepted and encouraged. There is also a gift shop which raises funds for maintenance.

DODGE COUNTY: Home of the Horicon Marsh

Dodge County claims Horicon Marsh, but the marsh also covers part of Fond du Lac County. Horicon Marsh may be Wisconsin's best bird-lover's paradise. It is the largest freshwater cattail marsh in the United States and is a bird refuge where more than 300 species have been identified. It is along the migratory route of many birds that stop to rest there every year. Millions of waterfowl pass through, including a quarter million Canada geese, among many others. As a result, it has been named a "Globally Important Bird Area," a designation from BirdLife International, and a "Wetland of International Importance," designated by the Ramsar Convention, an international treaty on wetlands. In addition to birds there are snakes, reptiles, small mammals, fish, and more. There are 22,000 acres that comprise the Horicon National Wildlife Refuge run by the U. S. Fish and Wildlife Service. An additional 11,000 acres south of that is Wisconsin's Horicon Marsh State Wildlife Area, managed by the state's Department of Natural Resources.

DODGEVILLE: Home of Wisconsin's Oldest Courthouse

Dodgeville is the county seat of Iowa County, in the southwestern part of the state where most of the early settlement of Wisconsin occurred. Iowa County came into existence in 1829 as part of the Michigan Territory and the original county seat was Mineral Point. Mineral Point remained the county seat when the county became part of the newly created Wisconsin Territory and when Wisconsin became a state in 1848. However, Dodgeville citizens wanted to move the county seat to their village and in 1858 county voters decided to move the county seat to Dodgeville as it was located close to the center of the county. A design for a new courthouse by Ernest Wiesen was selected, and construction began in 1859. Its architecture is Greek Revival and it was built out of locally sourced Galena limestone. There was some debate about whether Dodgeville should be the county seat or whether it should stay with Mineral Point even after the vote, but it was decided with certainty by voters in another election in 1861. While there have been additions and renovations to the building since it was first built, the building has been in continuous use since its construction. In 1972, it was added to the National Register of Historic Places.

DOUSMAN: Home of the Wisconsin Frog Jump

When the town was founded in the latter part of the 19th century it was officially named Dousman, but many referred to it as Bullfrog Station because of the surrounding marshes, bogs, and large population of frogs. Reflecting this, there are businesses in the town that use Bullfrog as a part of their name and the water tower has a frog painted on it. The town's welcome sign shows a bullfrog on a lily pad and notes it is the home of the Wisconsin State Frog Jump. The jump was patterned after the more famous Calaveras County frog jump written about by Mark Twain. It has been held every year since 1955 during the annual village festival, Derby Days. For those who don't have their own frogs, there are frogs available to rent for the contest. The frogs are released after the event. The record jump was in 1974 and was 19 feet and 3 ½ inches.

DUNDEE: UFO Capital of the World

Apparently there are a lot of UFO sightings in Wisconsin. Belleville and Elmwood vie for the right to the title of UFO Capital of Wisconsin, while Dundee goes for the big one and proclaims itself UFO Capital of the World (and sometimes of Wisconsin). Aside from these three there have been reported UFO sightings in many of the state's cities and towns. In Dundee, two people witnessed a circular object hovering over a neighbor's farm back in 1985. It was said the object frightened the cows below it. There have been other sightings since then, mostly around nearby Dundee Mountain in the Kettle Moraine State Forest. There have also been reports of crop circles appearing on farms around the area. Dundee and the surrounding area revel in the other-worldly visitors. For many years, starting in 1988, there was an annual gathering called UFO Daze and, according to Roadside America, the citizens put up landing lights along Highway 67 to encourage alien visitors from places other than Illinois. UFO Daze was held at a bar named Benson's Hideaway in nearby Campbellsport on Long Lake. The bar had a UFO theme with posters, aliens, and even a glass jar holding what the owner, Bill Benson, claimed was a small, preserved alien. Benson passed away in 2021 and UFO Daze ended with him. In 2018 filmmaker Mark Borhcardt released a short documentary, *The Dundee Project*, about UFO Daze and the local UFO craze.

E

EAGLE RIVER: Snowmobile Capital of the World

Located in the forests of northern Wisconsin Eagle River gets a large amount of snow every year and the people there have taken advantage of that by creating more than 500 miles of snowmobile trails. Upkeep of the trails is managed by volunteers from several area snowmobiling clubs. As home of the annual World Championship Snowmobile Derby every January, the town has laid claim as the Snowmobile Capital of the World. The derby started in the 1960s, so there are decades of history associated with it. The event draws tens of thousands of visitors every year. Eagle River is also the location of the World Snowmobile Headquarters, which in turn is home of the International Snowmobile Hall of Fame, the World Championship Wall of Fame, and the Snowmobile Museum. The museum houses displays on many aspects of snowmobiles and snowmobiling history and highlights a wide variety of snowmobiles including antiques, racers, minis, and more.

EAU CLAIRE: Horseradish Capital of the World
               Kubb Capital of North America

Eau Claire bills itself as the Horseradish Capital of the World. There is a city in Illinois and one in California that make the same claim. The Eau Claire area is in fact one of the nation's leading growers of horseradish. While less is grown in Eau Claire than in Collinsville, Illinois, which produces a great majority of the world's supply, there is greater production of horseradish for *domestic* supply in Eau Claire. The Collinsville area exports much of theirs. The horseradish business in the Eau Claire area started in 1929 when a traveling lightning rod salesman, Ellis Huntsinger, was struck by an idea and decided to stop traveling and start farming. He planted a few acres, including some horseradish, which he found grows well in northern climates. The horseradish part of his farm took root, so to speak, and he was able to bottle and sell his horseradish locally. The operation became Silver Spring Foods, which these days is run by a fourth generation of the family and is the largest grower and processor of horseradish in the world.

Eau Claire also lays claim as the Kubb Capital of North America. Kubb is a lawn game that originated in Sweden. It has been described as a combination of bowling, bocce, and horseshoes. The goal is to throw batons in an attempt to knock down opponents' kubbs, which are wooden blocks placed on opposite sides of the field, or pitch. Once a team knocks down all of their opponents' kubbs they then have to knock down the king, a larger block of wood placed in the center of the pitch, to win the game. While its origins may date back a thousand years, the modern game has been around for just a few decades. Kubb regained popularity in Sweden, particularly on the island of Gotland, in the 1980s. It spread to other countries in Europe in the 2000s. In 2007 Eric and Erin Anderson, who loved the game and had recently moved to Eau Claire, decided to host a tournament as a fundraiser. It grew from 35 players that first year to more than 120 teams and 400 competitors within a decade and from a local fundraiser to a Midwest Championship to the U. S. championship. The City Council declared Eau Claire the Kubb Capital of North America in 2011.

EDGERTON: Tobacco Capital of the World
              Boyhood Home of Sterling North

A lot of people don't know that Wisconsin, particularly the southern part, has historically produced a large amount of tobacco, going back to the mid-1800s. Tobacco farming grew during the Civil War as most tobacco was grown in the southern states prior to the war. Production in southern Wisconsin peaked in the early to mid-1900s when considerably more was grown than what the area produces now. Driving down country roads one can see many tobacco sheds, also known as tobacco barns. They are long structures with slats for ventilation where the tobacco is dried. Wisconsin tobacco has mostly been used for chewing tobacco or wrapping cigars rather than smoking, although in recent years those who are still planting the crop have been growing tobacco for pipes and cigarettes as well. While there are a handful of farmers still growing and selling tobacco in Edgerton, the industry seems to be winding down. There is a lot of tobacco history, and it is evident everywhere as there are old tobacco warehouses all over Edgerton. At one time there were around 50 of them and a dozen or so operating tobacco companies. In recognition of that history, there is an annual Tobacco Heritage Festival sponsored by local businesses and the Wisconsin Leaf Tobacco Dealers. How long this event will continue with the current climate around tobacco remains to be seen.

Writer Sterling North was born just a few miles out of Edgerton and grew up in the town. The house where he grew up is now a museum and the home of the Sterling North Society. It is listed on the National Register of Historic Places. North started his career as a journalist and later turned to writing novels. His most famous book, *Rascal,* was released in 1963 and told the story about a boy spending a year raising a racoon, touching upon other subjects such as relationships and transitions. The book's subtitle was "A memoir of a better era." It became one of the best-selling children's books of all time and won numerous awards, including the Newberry medal. It was turned into a Disney movie in 1969.

ELKHART LAKE: Home of the World's Largest Barber Pole
                  Home of Road America

About a mile or so out of Elkhart Lake is what is claimed to be the world's largest barber pole. It is actually something seen on farms all over Wisconsin—a silo—but painted with red, white, and blue stripes to look like a barber pole, and with good reason. At the base of the silo and next to a barn is a small building that used to be the milkhouse, but was converted into a functioning barbershop. The business is appropriately called The Barber Pole. The owner, David Gumieny, had the pole painted during the bicentennial year of 1976. The shop and the pole have been featured on numerous local and national television shows.

Elkhart Lake is better known as the home of Road America, America's National Park of Speed. Built in the 1950s, the Road America racetrack has hosted over 500 events a year, including IndyCar, Trans-Am series, and NASCAR races, among others. NASCAR decided to move its Cup series from Road America to Chicago city streets as of 2023. Prior to the building of the Road America track, races were held on public county highways and Elkhart Lake streets until legislation made that illegal. The original public highway course is listed on the National Register of Historic Places. The track at Road America is considered one of the world's best and toughest tracks and was even voted the Best NASCAR Track in America in 2021, which makes the move to Chicago just two years later a bit surprising. It is a four-mile course with fourteen turns through hills and ravines in the Kettle Moraine area of Wisconsin. The Department of Transportation even offers a special Road America license plate for fans.

ELKHORN: Christmas Card Town
                Home of the Beast of Bray Road

Back in 1952, Elkhorn was featured on a television program called "March of Time." The program showcased the town during the Christmas holiday season. It got the attention of an executive with Ford, who several years later hired artist Cecile Johnson to create six Christmas paintings using Elkhorn as the backdrop for the watercolors. These were used to illustrate an article on the holiday. The paintings, in turn, caught the eye of a greeting card company which used five of the six on Christmas cards that sold widely and gave the town its nickname. The original paintings are on display at Elkhorn's City Hall. The city has continued to sponsor a new painting every year, and the collection is housed at the public library. The city hosts an annual Christmas Card Town holiday parade every December, featuring floats, bands, and a visit from Santa and Mrs. Claus.

Elkhorn doesn't necessarily promote the Beast of Bray Road, but articles, a book, television shows, a documentary, and a horror movie have been made about it. It has been called several other names, including the Wisconsin Werewolf. The man-beast is a wolf-like creature with human features that has been spotted around Bray Road in Elkhorn since the 1930s, with a number of new reports around Elkhorn and other parts of southeastern Wisconsin in the late 20th century. It is said to be able to walk on all fours or upright and has a furry human body with canine features. It is thought that residents may be confusing it with a real animal, such as a wolf, due to the witness descriptions of the beast. Others believe it is Bigfoot and still others think it is an as yet unidentified animal. An annual Beast of Bray Road Festival was started in Elkhorn in 2020. While the city has put up no signs about the beast several residents along Bray Road have placed wood carvings and other images of it in their yards.

ELLSWORTH: Cheese Curd Capital of Wisconsin

Who can resist the taste of quality cheese curds that squeak when you eat them? Wisconsinites know that if they don't squeak they are not the best. Named the Cheese Curd Capital of Wisconsin with a 1984 proclamation by Governor Tony Earl, those squeaky curds are celebrated in Ellsworth with an annual Cheese Curd Festival during the last week of June. In addition, cheese curd banners adorn Main Street. Besides the parade and typical festival events like runs and walks, there is a cheese curd eating contest, cheese curd food dishes, and thousands of pounds of cheese curds available to visitors to eat on the festival grounds or take home to enjoy later. Free samples of one of Wisconsin's favorite foods are offered by the Ellsworth Cooperative Creamery, a cheese-making business in existence since 1910. A mural on the creamery shows a bucolic farm scene and proclaims Ellsworth the Cheese Curd Capital of Wisconsin. The cooperative produces over 150,000 pounds of cheese curds every day and is the reason the town earned its capital title.

ELMWOOD: UFO Capital of Wisconsin

This is a contested title. Belleville and Dundee also bill themselves as the UFO Capital of Wisconsin due to a number of sightings in each of the towns. Dundee also claims to be the UFO Capital of the World. In Elmwood's story, the first UFO sighting was reported by a police officer, George Wheeler, who claimed to see what looked like a comet, a fiery red light streaking across the sky. About a year later, Wheeler reported another sighting of a large bright light that he thought was a fire at first. When he investigated it he called in a UFO sighting, reporting a silver craft about 250 feet across with a bright light coming from the top. As he told it later, while he was on the radio the craft rose up and a blue ray or flash caused his car's engine to cut out. His radio also went out and he lost contact with the dispatcher. He was later found uninjured in the squad car, but apparently weak, with no lights on the car and burned-out spark plugs. Other citizens reported seeing the light that same night and some reported televisions going out about the same time. For a couple of years there were so many sightings in Elmwood that Tom Weber of Chippewa Falls proposed building a UFO landing strip. The idea was supported by local businesspeople and city leaders although it was, at least in part, considered as much for attracting tourists as aliens. Weber was not able to raise enough money and the multi-million-dollar project never came to fruition. Like Belleville, the

UFO title is celebrated with a festival every year. In Elmwood it is called UFO Days.

EPHRAIM: The Last Dry Town in Wisconsin

Ephraim was founded by a zealous Norwegian Moravian minister, Reverend Andreas Iverson, and his followers. It was named for a Biblical word that means "fruitful," and was founded as a dry town. Though the tourist packets never went out of their way to tell potential visitors about it, Ephraim has been labeled as The Last Dry Town in Wisconsin. Years ago, many towns were "dry," meaning alcoholic beverages could not be sold within the township. Little by little, laws got more lax and dry towns became wet towns. Given that Wisconsin consistently leads the nation or is near the top in consumption of both beer and brandy, it's not surprising that towns switched from dry to wet over the years. Many of its cities land on drunkest cities lists and the state almost aways tops the lists of drunkest states. The conversion of towns from dry to wet could easily have been predicted. However, citizens of Ephraim held on to the old ways much longer than most. They voted to remain dry in 1934 with 59% of the vote and as late as 1992 by just under a three to one margin. In 1994, Richland Center and Port Edwards became wet by votes of their citizens, leaving Ephraim as The Last Dry Town in Wisconsin. It was 22 years later with another vote that Ephraim citizens finally voted to end their history as a dry town. A referendum on allowing beer sales passed 127-98 and wine sales passed with a vote of 152-73, ending 163 years as a dry town.

EVANSVILLE: Soybean Capital of Wisconsin

Evansville has a proud farming tradition, with soybeans as one of the two big cash crops in the area, along with corn. In a nod to area farmers and the importance of soybean crops, the Wisconsin Soybean Association officially designated the city as the Soybean Capital of Wisconsin in 2007. The state of Wisconsin also issued a proclamation with the same designation. Local officials put up signs that year proudly proclaiming the title of Soybean Capital. Besides the importance of soybean crops to the local economy, the designation was due in large part to a proposed biodiesel plant that never materialized. The facility would have converted oils extracted from area soybeans into fuel. The State of Wisconsin provided a quarter million-dollar grant and construction was started on the plant, but it was unexpectedly halted a year later. The company that would have built and operated the plant, North Prairie Productions, decided to drop the project due to high commodity prices which would have lowered their expected profits. For large corporations, what is best for the communities in which they operate is always less important than the profits they can make.

EXELAND: Trout Fishing Capital of Wisconsin

Trout fish sandwiches, a trout fishing contest (brook trout only, please), and the crowning of the Trout Festival Queen and Little Princess are among the highlights of the annual Exeland Trout Festival, honoring the town's reputation as the Trout Fishing Capital of Wisconsin. Exeland is located in Sawyer County, which has dozens of lakes, rivers, and streams for fishing. Area fishing spots around Exeland include Beverly Lake, Borido Lake, Brunet River, Couderay River, Jacques Lake, Kenyon Creek, and Swan Creek. There are a number of other streams a little further away as well. There are several fishing resorts and fishing guides in the surrounding area.

F

FENNIMORE: Home of the Dinky

It's not just a strange claim to fame. It has meaning. A dinky is a short railroad line. The Dinky in Fennimore was a narrow-gauge Chicago and Northwestern train that traveled between Fennimore and Woodman on a daily run around the latter part of the 19th and early part of the 20th centuries. It provided an important transportation link for the people of the area at a time before most people had access to cars and trucks. In addition to passengers, it hauled mail and other freight. The original Dinky, Old Faithful # 279, is long gone from Fennimore and is now on display in the small town of Pioche, Nevada, A similar train was secured and is on display at the Fennimore Railroad Historical Society Museum. The train currently in Fennimore is a 1907 Davenport 2-6-0 locomotive.

Today, the old train is honored with the Dinky Trail, a bike trail that very closely follows the route of the original narrow-gauge line. Bicyclists travel between the railroad museum in Fennimore and the Dinky General Store in Woodman, an old-fashioned general store with a railroad theme.

FISH CREEK: Home of America's Oldest Resident Summer Theater

Fish Creek is located on the beautiful peninsula known as Door County. Because of its natural beauty, coastline, and lighthouses, the entire peninsula is a haven for tourists and artists. To hear that Fish Creek is the home of the oldest continuous professional summer stock theater company in the country fits in well with the artistic and tourist-oriented bent of the county. The name of the group, appropriately enough, is the Peninsula Players and they have been performing since 1935. Their first production was *Hay Fever*, by Noel Coward. In 1937, the company purchased a former boys' camp and built a new theater there in a cedar forest setting with walking paths that lead to views of Green Bay (the bay, not the city). Performances are held outdoors and patrons are protected from inclement weather by a roof over the seating. Along with the Peninsula Players, the county is home to numerous other arts groups, including Door Shakespeare, Northern Sky Theater (formerly American Folklore Theatre), Peninsula School of Art, Peninsula Players Theatre, Peninsula Music Festival, Fishstock Concert Series, the Door County Auditorium, and more.

FORT ATKINSON: Home of the National Dairy Shrine Visitors' Center

What better place for a dairy museum than in the heart of America's Dairyland? The National Dairy Shrine is an organization dedicated to dairy farming and includes farmers, educators, manufacturers, and others who have an interest in all aspects of the industry. The organization and its Visitors' Center and Museum are located in Fort Atkinson. It was built next to the already existing Hoard Historical Museum and construction was completed in 1981. Appropriately, the neighboring local history museum was named after William Dempster Hoard, a former Wisconsin governor and the man considered to be the father of the Wisconsin dairy industry. He created Hoard's Dairyman magazine, which is still published, and was an early promoter of scientific farming. The Dairy Shrine gives a glimpse into the past, present, and possible future of dairy farming. Scads of dairy artifacts are on display, as well as photographs of famous dairy cows and portraits of dairy farmers in the Dairy Hall of Fame. There are Elsie artifacts galore, as well as tributes to other famous cows. The center also houses the Joe Eves Library with hundreds of dairy-related books.

FOUNTAIN CITY: Home of the Rock in the House
Home of Prairie Moon Sculpture Garden
Home of Kinstone

Wisconsin not only has the famous House on the Rock near Spring Green, but also is home to the Rock in the House in Fountain City. In 1995 a two-story tall 55-ton boulder rolled down a steep Mississippi River bluff and crashed into the back of a newly remodeled house where it startled the owners (or maybe scared the bejesus out of them) when it lodged into the back of the building. The house was owned by Dwight and Maxine Anderson, who soon sold it to real estate developer John Burt. They moved to another house, the boulder stayed where it was, and Burt turned it into a tourist attraction. For a long time, the house interior had been open to visitors on the honor system. Signs directed tourists to deposit a requested $2.00 donation into a cashbox. Visitors can no longer go inside the house after someone stole the cashbox, which was probably worth more than the amount of money in it. Tourists are now welcome to walk around the house exterior to view the boulder still lodged inside the back of it. Oddly enough, a previous house that stood immediately next to the Rock in the House was hit by a five-ton boulder in 1901. That boulder caused the couple, Mr. and Mrs. Dubler, to drop from their bedroom into the cellar. Mrs. Dubler was killed, likely instantaneously, while her blind husband who had been sleeping next to her escaped unscathed except for a small bruise on his forehead. Unlike the Rock in the House dwelling, the Dubler house was demolished.

Prairie Moon Sculpture Garden is one of the incredible sculpture parks created by untrained and driven artists around Wisconsin. These self-taught artists have created hundreds of sculptures with no artistic training, but with creativity and passion. Most of the work at Prairie Moon Sculpture Garden was created by Herman Rusch, who built 40 sculptures after he retired in 1952. Several years after first retiring he built his first piece and did not stop until he had created dozens. Like several of these sites around the Badger State, the Kohler Foundation helped to save and restore Rusch's work. Unlike the other sites, Prairie Moon includes work by a couple other folk artists.

Kinstone is a Midwest Stonehenge. It is billed as a "modern megalithic garden" and is a 30-acre site filled with sculptures, megaliths, a labyrinth, and a chapel for prayer and meditation. For most people the highlight of the site is the Great Stone Circle. It is over 18 feet in diameter and is a circle of 19 megaliths. The tallest is over 30 feet and the heaviest is more than 70,000 pounds. The circle and other sculptures are designed for the sun to align with specific spots during solstice and equinox times. Kinstone is privately owned and the owner offers various tours, retreats, classes, and workshops. A guided tour is not required. Visitors can wander the site at their own pace. There is a gift shop onsite.

FOX LAKE: Home of Bunny Berigan

While he may be little known now, Bunny Berigan was one of the most well-respected musicians in the early part of the 20th century. The popular trumpet player and bandleader was born in Hilbert, Wisconsin as Bernard Berigan, but the family moved to Fox Lake when Bunny Berigan was just a few months old. As a child he played in the Fox Lake Juvenile Band and as a teenager he started playing professionally. As an adult, he was known as one of the greatest jazz trumpeters of all time, playing with such greats as Benny Goodman, the Dorsey Brothers, Rudee Valley, Glenn Miller, Billie Holiday, and Bing Crosby. He also played violin. Berigan was a highly sought-after studio musician, playing on hundreds of recordings in the 1930s. He later started his own orchestra and scored big with his theme song and hit, "I Can't Get Started." Unfortunately, he died in 1942 at only 33 years old of complications from alcoholism and cirrhosis, which put an early end to his rise in the music industry. He is buried at St. Mary's/Annunciation Cemetery in Fox Lake. The Bunny Berigan Jazz Jubilee was held in Fox Lake for many years beginning in the early 1970s, but after the 2018 event the jubilee folded due to funding issues. There is a Wisconsin historical marker about Berigan at Adams Springs Park in Fox Lake.

FRANKSVILLE: The Cabbage Capital of the World
                Home of the World Sauerkraut Eating Contest

If you're not a fan of the taste or smell of sauerkraut it might be hard to understand Franksville's sauerkraut eating contest, but knowing that Wisconsin is heavily German in heritage helps to make it more understandable. Franksville was once home to the Fremont Company, which manufactured Frank's Sauerkraut. The company was started in 1907. The business was purchased by an Ohio company and the sauerkraut plant closed down in 1985. Local manufacturing facilities are often shuttered after being purchased by out-of-state companies. Cabbage and sauerkraut were so important to the community prior to the sale there is even a business named Cabbage Heads Tavern and Grill. Every year from 1950 for about 50 years, Franksville's Kraut Festival hosted what they claimed was the world's only sauerkraut eating contest. The festival originally started as s company picnic, but grew into an annual celebration that helped raise funds for local organizations. The event was always in late June, but the celebration died away within a few years after the factory closed. In 2015 a new festival was begun called the Kraut Music Festival. There are still a good number of area farms growing cabbage.

FREISTADT: Home of Wisconsin's Oldest Lutheran Church

Founded in 1839 Freistadt was home to a group of Lutherans who came to Wisconsin to escape persecution in their Pomeranian homeland. The Prussian king who controlled the area at that time had made Lutheranism illegal, so many of the adherents decided to flee to America. Freistadt translates from the German as Free City. In the spring of 1840, less than half a year after their arrival, they had already constructed their first church, a log cabin building where the immigrants could freely worship. It also served as the first Lutheran

Church school in the state. The original building is gone and there is now a log cabin where it once stood, next to the current Trinity Lutheran Church. The site is home to a living history museum with a blacksmith shop, a barn in its original location, other historical buildings, and antique farm implements. Freistadt itself is now a neighborhood in the city of Mequon.

FREMONT: White Bass Capital of the World

According to the Fremont Area Chamber of Commerce website there is a large spawning run of white bass every spring and again in the fall, with limitless fish to be caught. Literally, there is no limit. You can catch as many as you can catch. The run typically lasts for several weeks. The town is nestled on the Wolf River, one of Wisconsin's great rivers, and Fremont is one of the fishing hot spots along the river. Aside from white bass the town and river boast loads of other bass, sturgeon, walleye, crappie, catfish, northern pike, and more. During the two spawning runs there are apparently almost as many people fishing as there are fish. There are so many who come during the white bass runs that it is almost impossible to get a room or campsite for miles around. If you do manage to secure a room, many of the resorts in the area have their own docks, so visitors can fish right from the place where they are staying. There are also several public docks where anglers can get their fill of the local white bass. There is a slightly earlier run for walleye. For the local fishing shops and bait shops, the spawning run in the spring is their busiest time of year, along with the fall run, and can help them survive the rest of the year.

G

GAYS MILLS: Apple Capital of Wisconsin

Located along the banks of the Kickapoo River, Gays Mills, with a population of just over 500 citizens, is home to half a dozen apple orchards where prize-winning apples are grown. In 1905 apples from the area won first prize at the Wisconsin State Fair and later won grand prize at a national show in New York state. Around that time, the Wisconsin Horticultural Society encouraged the planting of more apple trees throughout the state. In Gays Mills there are now over 1,000 acres devoted to apple growing. It is the largest concentration of orchards in the tri-state area (Wisconsin, Minnesota, and Iowa). The orchards grow multiple varieties and typically sell products such as apple cider, caramel apples, apple jelly, and other farm products. Customers can buy apples directly from the orchards or make it an outing and pick their own apples. Hundreds of people are employed to harvest apples during the summer and early fall. In September there is an annual Apple Fest to celebrate the apple's importance to the local economy.

GERMANTOWN: Deutschstadt

Deutschstadt translates as German city or, in this case, Germantown, which gives a fairly good idea that this town takes pride in its German heritage. The Deutschstadt Heritage Foundation hosts an annual fundraiser called Mai Fest and uses the proceeds to benefit the community and help preserve its German heritage. Mai Fest is a celebration of spring. The festival is held in Germany and anywhere worldwide where German people have settled. In the fall, the town celebrates Oktoberfest, another popular festival in Germany and around the world. Look for German food, music, and dancing at both events, even including a dance around the Maipole in spring. Many of the early settlers in the area came from Germany, starting in the 1840s and, like many cities in Wisconsin, their traditions have been passed down for generations.

GLEASON: Trout Fishing Capital of the World

Located on the Prairie River, considered to be a good trout stream, the town of Gleason prides itself on the native brook trout that can be caught there. It is the only stream trout native to Wisconsin. Other area streams provide great trout fishing as well as other fish species. The state record brook trout was caught in the Prairie River. It was nine pounds, 15 ounces and was caught on September 2, 1944. That record still stands. Fisher's Bar in Gleason has a replica of the fish on display. Like "the one that got away" the original was lost. It sounds like a bit of a fish story, but the record fish was officially measured and recorded at the time. Teachers at the local elementary school worked wih their students to paint two signs proclaiming Gleason as the Trout Capital of the World. They were placed on the highway coming into town from both directions. The southbound one was removed by the Department of Natural Resources and destroyed because it was erected on public land without permission, which seems like a bit of a harsh response to a local school project. The northbound one still stands.

GLIDDEN: Black Bear Capital of the World
          Black Bear Capital of Wisconsin
          Home of the World's Largest White Pine Log

If one wants to see bears in Wisconsin there is only one way to go—north. And Glidden is about as far north as it gets. Located in Ashland County, Glidden is proud that the world's record black bear was shot and killed near the town. Taken in 1963 the bear was estimated to be 12 years old. It was seven feet, ten inches tall, 665 pounds dressed, and gave the town its claim to fame. It took seven men to drag it out of the woods about five miles east of the town. The record has been broken since then, which is likely why the town is now more likely called the Black Bear Capital of Wisconsin instead of The World. The former record-holding stuffed bear is memorialized as a display in a glass case next to the town hall in Glidden. It is affectionately known as Mr. Bear by the locals and the school made the black bear its mascot. A sign at the entrance to the town has a black bear on it and there is also one painted on the water tower.

Considerably larger than Mr. Bear, the World's Largest White Pine Log is also said to be the last one sleigh hauled. It still sits on the sleigh that brought it to Glidden and is on display in Marion Park. The log is 20 feet long, weighs 7,000 pounds, and is estimated to be somewhere between 500 and 600 years old. It could create a great amount of lumber, but Glidden has decided to keep it on display right where it is.

GRAND CHUTE: Home of the John Birch Society
                Birthplace of Joseph McCarthy

Originally founded as a response to Communism, the John Birch

Society is a conservative organization that believes in and educates the public about their perceived need for less government. Members also believe that the U. S. government is founded upon rights given to us by God, not men, and it supports strong Christian influence on government. Founded in 1958 by Robert Welch, the organization and its magazine, *The New American*, are both based in the Appleton suburb of Grand Chute. The John Birch Society's influence waned for quite some time, but saw a resurgence in the early 2000s, and is now reflected in the right-wing faction of the modern Republican party.

While the city doesn't really promote it, Joseph McCarthy, the Commie-hunting Wisconsin Senator who headed the House Un-American Activities Committee back in the 1950s, was born on a farm outside of Grand Chute. In 1936, he lost his first bid for public office running as a Democrat for District Attorney while living in Shawano. Winning his first election in 1939 in a non-partisan race he became the youngest circuit judge ever elected in Wisconsin. After service in World War II McCarthy switched parties and became a Republican, losing his first race for the Senate. Several years later he won election to the United State Senate at only 38 years old. He went on to fame as the Communist witch-hunter of the 1950s. During his time in the Senate, he became famous (and infamous) for accusing politicians, artists, government employees, and others of being Communists or having Communist sympathies. His accusations, most of which had no basis in fact, destroyed many careers and reputations and his name came to be associated with those who would recklessly accuse others of wrongdoing with little or no proof. There is no marker at his birthplace and no statues of him in Grand Chute, although there is a bronze bust of him in the History Museum at the Castle in Appleton. It was dedicated in 1959 and was on display in the Outagamie County Courthouse until 2001 when it was donated to the museum. The only other monument to McCarthy is his gravesite at St. Mary's Cemetery which has been visited over the years by both admirers and vandals.

GRANTSBURG: Home of Big Gust

Big Gust was not a powerful wind, but a powerful man. An immigrant from Sweden, he settled in Grantsburg where he was known as the world's largest policeman. Born Anders Gustaf Anderson in 1872, he grew to be seven and a half feet tall and weighed more than 350 pounds. He became a United States citizen in 1902, the same year the town hired him as their marshal. He had previously worked as a policeman in Superior. In Grantsburg, Gust took on many roles and was well-liked and respected by his fellow citizens. He served as a policeman, head of the local fire department, assessor, road supervisor, lamplighter, and dog catcher for the town until he passed away in 1926. A life-sized wooden sculpture created by Alf Manley Olson in 1980 was put in a glass case in front of the community center on Pine Street to honor him. Visitors can press a button to listen to his story. In addition, the town hosts an annual Big Gust Days festival the first weekend of June.

GREEN BAY: Wisconsin's Oldest City
               Titletown U. S. A.
               Toilet Paper Capital of the World
               Home of the World's Largest Hex Nut

Green Bay has several titles, which is appropriate for a city that has Titletown, U. S. A. as one of its titles. Citizens who are sports fans are undoubtedly most proud of the Titletown title. The nickname is a reference to the National Football League champion Green Bay Packers. The football team is owned by individual citizens rather than one or more rich people, the only team in major professional sports that is publicly owned. The Packers won six championships under Coach Curly Lambeau, after whom the stadium is named, between 1929 and 1944. They won another five championships under Coach Vince Lombardi between 1961 and 1968, including the first two Super Bowls. The team won the Super Bowl again in 1997 under Coach Mike Holmgren and again in 2011 under Coach Mike McCarthy. Near Lambeau Field is Titletown, a recreation park that offers restaurants, athletic fields, an ice skating rink, and much more for visitors to enjoy.

Those who like their history are probably a little prouder of the city being considered Wisconsin's oldest, though this doesn't take into account Native American settlements that had been in existence for years before any white men began settling in the state. French explorer Jean Nicolet came across the area in 1634 and named it

Green Bay due to the color of the water in the bay. By 1655 a trading post had been established, making it not only Wisconsin's oldest city, but one of the oldest permanent European settlements anywhere in the country.

Undoubtedly there are some citizens who are neither fans of sports nor history, who are perhaps most proud of the Toilet Paper Capital of the World title, particularly if they work in Green Bay's paper industry. There are many paper companies in Wisconsin's northern tier, including one of the nation's largest, Quilted Northern (formerly just Northern), in Green Bay. Also, the first splinter-free toilet paper was developed in the city in 1935, which changed the course (coarse?) of toilet paper history. Previously, toilet paper was made from wood chips and although it was pulped and treated there would occasionally be splinters in it. This might explain why the Sears catalogue was kept in outhouses back in the day. Northern made toilet paper safer and advertised it as splinter free and became a leading manufacturer as a result, presumably much to the relief of the Sears catalogue publishers. The paper industry in the county, including toilet paper, employs thousands of people at a couple dozen paper mills.

The World's Largest Hex Nut is a stainless-steel hex nut that stands ten feet tall in front of Packer Fastener on Lombardi Avenue. It was built by employees of the company to promote the business. It stands near the company slogan, "We have the biggest nuts in town," which is on a banner in front of the building. No more needs to be said.

GREEN COUNTY: America's Little Switzerland

Green County as a whole considers itself America's Little Switzerland, primarily because of a large influx of Swiss settlers around New Glarus in August of 1845. The settlers were from Glarus, Switzerland and named their community New Glarus, which also bills itself as America's Little Switzerland (see New Glarus). Meanwhile, Monroe is considered the Swiss Cheese Capital (see Monroe). The entire area, though, has a strong Swiss influence. After the initial settlement of New Glarus more immigrants came from other parts of the Swiss homeland and settled in the area, which strongly resembles the hills of their home country. There are still people in the county who speak the German-Swiss dialect and many more who still celebrate their heritage in many other ways. You may find folks in a bar playing a Swiss card game called Jass (pronounced with a Y sound), or hear a band playing traditional Swiss folk music. It's likely one of the only places in the United States where a person might hear authentic yodeling or the playing of an alpenhorn. While in Green County, you can buy souvenir tee-shirts, albums, pins, and more labeled Swissconsin.

GREEN LAKE: Home of the Deepest Lake in Wisconsin
                        Wisconsin's Lake Trout Capital

At seven miles wide and a maximum depth of 237 feet, Green Lake, also called Big Green Lake, is considered the deepest inland lake in Wisconsin. The average depth is 100 feet. There is oxygen all the way to the bottom of the lake, which makes for prime habitat for lake trout, though the dissolved oxygen levels have been depleting for years. The Wisconsin state record lake trout was caught in Green Lake, as was the state record cisco. The trout was caught by Joseph Gotz in 1957 and weighed 35 pounds, four ounces. The lake trout season runs from early January through the end of September. An inland trout stamp is required when fishing for lake trout. Many other fish species also make the lake home, including walleye, northern pike, white bass, and muskies, among others. There are more than three dozen species of fish in the lake. Several local fishing guides are available. In February, there is an annual WinterFest on the lake which features an ice fishing trout derby where fishers try to catch the largest lake trout and maybe set a new state record.

H

HAUGEN: Mushroom and Kolache Capital

Haugen is one of the smallest capitals in Wisconsin, with a population of less than 300 people, yet it promotes a combined title. There are several cities in America that lay claim to being kolache or mushroom capitals, but Haugen is the only one that claims both. Kolaches are sweet fruit pastries that originated in what is now the Czech Republic and were brought to the United States by Bohemian settlers in the Haugen area and elsewhere. The word kolache comes from a Czech and Old Slavonic word kola, meaning circle or wheel. Kolaches are round pastries with fruit fillings in the middle surrounded by a puffy dough.

Mushrooms are also an important part of Czech cooking and culture and are often incorporated into holiday or special occasion meals. Many foods in different cultures, including mushrooms in Czech culture, have been considered the "meat of the poor." Mushrooms and kolaches are the only images on the Haugen centennial logo from 2018, as well as other posters, buttons, and advertising promoting Haugen's annual Fun Days throughout the years. Among the highlights of Fun Days is the ethnic food and the naming of the Kolache Queen.

HAYWARD: Home of the Lumberjack World Championships
        Muskie Capital of the World
        Home of the National Freshwater Fishing Hall of
Fame
        Golf Capital of Wisconsin

Hayward is one heck of a place. Originally a lumbering town it is now a bustling tourist mecca, with as many Indian trading posts and fudge stores as Wisconsin Dells. Its lumberjacking origins are preserved and honored with the internationally recognized Lumberjack World Championships where people from all over the world compete in events such as birling (logrolling), speed climbing, chopping, axe tossing, and more. There are more than 20 events in all, over a three-day weekend. The event started in 1960 and has always been hosted at Hayward's Lumberjack Bowl. The bowl hosts lumberjack shows throughout the summer tourism season.

Along with the tourism that replaced logging camps came fishing and Hayward lays claim as Muskie Capital of the World. Boulder Junction claims to be the Musky Capital of the World and won a trademark battle against Hayward for rights to the name in court. The two cities had vied for the title, so the different spellings allow the two claims to co-exist. Hayward certainly makes an effort to prove its claim, with an annual Musky Festival, which includes a fly-fishing musky tournament. Cal Johnson caught a world record musky in Hayward back in July of 1949 which is still on the wall at the

Moccasin Bar. The record didn't last long as Louis Spray beat the record in October of 1949 with a 69-pound, 11-ounce musky that was over 60 inches long. It is still recognized as the world record. The record trophy fish was destroyed in a fire, and a replica of the fish is on display at the National Freshwater Fishing Hall of Fame.

No one can deny that Hayward is home to the world's largest musky, a huge fiberglass fish on the grounds of the National Freshwater Fishing Hall of Fame. It is four and half stories tall and over 140 feet long. It is so large its lower mouth forms an observation deck where a large family can all stand at one time and have their picture taken while they look out over the grounds. A number of other fiberglass fish of various species can be seen from the musky's mouth. The Hall of Fame is located in a separate building. Inside the hall are hundreds of outboard motors, lures, rods, reels, creels, mounted fish, photographs, and the official records of freshwater fishing.

Hayward also claims to be the Golf Capital of Wisconsin. With more than a dozen golf courses within an hour's drive (eight 18-hole courses and five nine-hole courses), seven of those in the immediate area, the city has claimed to be Wisconsin's golf capital since 1997. And this doesn't even count the mini-golf courses.

In addition to the above claims to fame, Hayward is the terminus for two races that are listed in this volume under the city of Cable. The American Birkebeiner cross country ski race and the Chequamegon 40, a mountain biking race (see the Cable listing for more information about these two events), both end on Main Street in Hayward.

HAZEL GREEN: The Point of Beginning

While this title doesn't make Hazel Green the capital or the home of anything, it really is an important distinction. What it refers to is the point just outside of town where the surveying of the state of Wisconsin was begun by Lucius Lyon and from which everything in the state was measured. According to the village website, "Today every property deed in Wisconsin includes a description which is based on the Point of Beginning (POB)." In 1831, 17 years before statehood, Lyon created a six square foot, six-foot-high marker on the spot. Surveying of public land started a year later from that spot.

Every lot, city or town, road, and more were mapped from this Point of Beginning. Lyon's marker disappeared sometime over the years, but there is now a concrete surveyors' monument at the site and a historical marker just south of the town.

HILLSBORO: Czech Capital of Wisconsin

The western border area of Wisconsin was one of the two areas in the state where Czech immigrants tended to congregate, the other being the Lake Michigan shoreline. While never the majority population, there were already close to 500 Czech settlers around the Hillsboro area in 1880, mostly from Bohemia and Moravia. They tended to hold onto their traditions, dress, and speech, so that even after the turn of the 20th century one could still hear Czech spoken in the town. Today, Hillsboro's Czech heritage is recalled every June with an event known as Cesky Den (Czech Day), where visitors can still sample some of the traditional foods, dances, and music of the early settlers. Available food includes kolaches, traditional noodle soup, and Czech sausages. The music includes Wisconsin's state dance, the polka. Czech polkas and music are played all day long and there is always a traditional polka Mass on the festival grounds.

HOLLANDALE: Home of Nick Engelbert's Grandview

Wisconsin has more than its share of eccentric folk artists. One of those was Nick Engelbert who created a number of sculptures on his property near Hollandale. An Austrian immigrant, he built about 40 sculptures in a couple of decades. The outside of his house, which was his first project, is covered with seashells, glass, beads, and even buttons. Engelbert worked in other media. Inside the house when the museum is open, visitors can see some of his paintings. Many of his sculptures had fallen into disrepair after he sold the property and left the state, but the current owners, the Pecatonica Educational Charitable Foundation, along with assistance from the Kohler Foundation, have worked to restore them. Onsite one can view Snow White and the Seven Dwarfs, Neptune's Fountain, a Norwegian sailor in a boat, animals, and more. Many of Engelbert's works have been in storage and are in the process of being restored so they can be returned to their original places on the property.

HUBERTUS: Home of Holy Hill National Shrine of Mary

Holy Hill is one of the most impressive religious sites in the state of Wisconsin, a Carmelite Basilica atop the highest elevation in southeastern Wisconsin and a 435-acre site that was sacred to Native Americans long before settlers arrived. The elevation is 1,330 feet above sea level, which for Wisconsin is high. The view from the top of the scenic tower is breathtaking, with miles of Kettle Moraine Forest spread out below. There is a story that a man known as the Hermit of Holy Hill, Francois Soubrio, was found living on the hill in the early 1860s. He had supposedly read that it was dedicated to the Virgin Mary and felt drawn to come from Canada to find the hill. The first chapel on the hill was built of logs in 1863, though it was known as a holy place and a place for meditation and prayer well before that. The current basilica was completed in 1931 and is now on the National Register of Historic Places. Today, pilgrims come from all over the world to visit the shrine, which is known as a place of healing and where one can see crutches and other aids left behind as evidence of a healed believer. There is even a story that the Hermit of Holy Hill himself had experienced a miraculous healing on the hill. Masses for the Catholic faithful are held daily.

HURLEY: Home of the World's Largest Corkscrew

The story is that during Prohibition, there were more than 100 places in Hurley, most of them on Silver Street, where people could go to get liquor, as well as other things such as companionship for an evening. There are no longer that many bars and the companionship may be a bit more difficult to find these days, too. There are still a couple dozen watering holes in the town, and a few places where one can go to buy liquor to take home. One of those is the Corkscrew Liquor Store along Highway 2, which is Home of the World's Largest corkscrew. The owner of the store and corkscrew collector, Gary Vittone, welded it himself from stainless steel tubing. The Guinness record for the largest corkscrew is for a five foot, eight-inch-long corkscrew made in Switzerland. Perhaps that record is for working corkscrews, as it apparently was able to function as a corkscrew on a large cork. The one in Hurley is 24 feet tall, but is more like a sculpture and not something that could actually open a wine bottle.

I

IRON RIVER: Blueberry Capital of the World

At one time there were a great many wild blueberries in the Iron River area, so many that visitors would come by train to pick them. While the blueberry crop isn't what it used to be there are still many berries to be had and the city is still known as the Blueberry Capital of the World. For about 60 years there has been an annual Blueberry Festival sponsored by the local Lions' Club. It is the club's biggest fundraising event. It seems that it's one of the rules of proclaiming a city the capital of something that there has to be a festival associated with the nickname. Wisconsin itself may very well be the nation's Festival Capital. The Blueberry Festival is always held the last weekend of July. Like many Wisconsin festivals this one includes a polka mass. Unlike others, there is an annual blueberry pie-eating contest and a blueberry pancake breakfast.

J

JACKSON COUNTY: Deer Capital of Wisconsin.

Jackson County and its county seat of Black River Falls both claim to be the Deer Capital of Wisconsin for the same reason— thousands of acres of prime hunting land in county and state forests, a large population of the state's official wildlife animal, the white-tailed deer, and hunters coming from all over the state and beyond to enjoy prime hunting. The deer hunting season in Wisconsin is big business and Jackson County is a significant contributor to that part of the state's economy.

JANESVILLE: Home of the Only Private Residence in Wisconsin Where Abraham Lincoln Slept
                    Home of Miracle, the White Buffalo

It's not "George Washington Slept Here," but it's the next best thing. The Lincoln-Tallman House is a Victorian home that gives one an idea of the things that wealth could buy in the 19th century. Built in 1857, it is now operated as a museum. Abraham Lincoln slept in the house in 1859. This was not his only visit to Wisconsin, however. In the early 1830s, as a Captain in the Black Hawk War, he would have slept all over southern Wisconsin, but in less splendorous surroundings. His visit to Janesville in October of 1859 followed speeches at the state fair in Milwaukee and another engagement in Beloit. William Tallman, the abolitionist owner of the house, had invited Lincoln to stay at his home in Janesville and as a result Lincoln added another speech in Janesville to his itinerary. The house is now owned by the Rock County Historical Society, which offers a number of different tours of the home.

In 1994 a white buffalo was born on a Janesville farm. It was named Miracle. For the Lakota, Dakota, and Nakota tribes, as well as other Native nations, the birth of a white calf is a prophetic sign of a return to harmony and balance, though the stories differ somewhat in detail. A white buffalo by itself would be interesting enough for most of us, but throw in the mystic qualities surrounding Miracle and it becomes fascinating. Miracle was not an albino and her fur turned black, red, and yellow over the course of a couple of years, which is also part of the Native prophesies. However, in the prophecies the last turn of color was to be brown, but Miracle died at ten years old before that part of the prophecy could be fulfilled. When she was alive many Native Americans, among others, traveled to the farm from all over the country. Thousands of people a day showed up to view or honor Miracle. The calf was born on the farm of Dave and Val Heider, who did not attempt to make money off of the white buffalo despite offers from many quarters to buy it or promote it. Instead, they allowed visitors to see it at no charge, although donations were accepted. Miracle died in 2004. Surprisingly, a second white buffalo was born on the same farm two years after Miracle's birth, but died after only three days. Amazingly, a third white buffalo was born on the same farm in 2006, just a couple of years after Miracle's passing. The last white buffalo born on the farm was a male and was named Miracle's Second Chance. It was struck by lightning and died just a few months after its birth.

JEFFERSON: The Gemuetlichkeit City

Another sign of Wisconsin's strong German heritage is the one welcoming visitors to Jefferson, the Gemuetlichkeit City. Gemuetlichkeit can be translated as "good times, good fun, and good fellowship," a warm and welcoming invitation for those who see the sign and know what it means. This is a rare instance when the celebration came not as a result of the town's nickname, but the other way around. Gemuetlichkeit Days started in 1971 as a celebration of the city's heavily German heritage and proved to be a popular annual celebration. The city later adopted "The Gemuetlichkeit City" as its nickname. Some of the activities that have been held at the festival are a bit different than most festivals around the state. Included are a children's stein carrying contest, euchre and sheepshead tournaments (both popular card games around Wisconsin), a Masskrugstemmen contest (a competition in which a filled stein must be held in an outstretched arm and the winner is the one who holds it the longest), nagelspiel (a German nail pounding contest), Find the Mecki (Mecki is a German cartoon hedgehog and this is a scavenger hunt for one item, a small Mecki doll), and polka lessons.

K

KAUKAUNA: Electric City

Most people who know the name Kaukauna know it because of their brand name cheese, but the town's name for itself is Electric City. The city built a hydroelectric plant on the Fox River in 1885, just three years after the first one in the world was built in nearby Appleton, as noted earlier in this book. Still, 1885 was early for hydroelectric power and it allowed Kaukauna to attract and keep industry and to adopt the nickname, Electric City, as its claim to fame. The city built several more hydroelectric plants over the years. Today, Kaukauna's hydroelectric history is honored with many businesses and organizations that include Electric City as part of their names, a beer named Electric City lager (from the Electric City Brewery), as well as an annual music festival, the Electric City Experience.

KENOSHA: Birthplace of Orson Welles

Often considered the greatest motion picture of all time, *Citizen Kane* was co-written, produced, and directed by the actor, writer, director, and producer Orson Welles, who also starred in the title role. Welles was born and spent his first few years in Kenosha. Welles is considered a great actor and one of the most innovative and greatest movie directors of all time. In his early years in the theater, he directed a 1937 production of *Macbeth* that featured all African American actors, the controversial *The Cradle Will Rock*, and others. Welles famously directed and narrated the radio play, *The War of the Worlds*, which convinced many listeners that we were being attacked by Martians. In addition to *Citizen Kane*, he was behind *The Magnificent Ambersons* and *The Lady from Shanghai*, among other films. Welles was born in a nondescript house that still exists on 7th Avenue. On the front yard, there is a lamp and next to it is a rock with a small plaque embedded in it that notes the house as the birthplace of Orson Welles, actor and director, with his birth and death dates. On the house is another small plaque from Kenosha's Historic Preservation Commission noting the house as his birthplace and also as Kenosha's landmark # 41.

KEWASKUM: Gateway to the Kettle Moraine
Birthplace of Glenway Wescott

The Kettle Moraine is a large state forest split into a northern, southern, and three other smaller units. A kettle is a depression formed by melting glacial ice. Often these get filled and become ponds or lakes. A moraine is a glacial deposit of rocks that form ridges. There are other geological features created by glaciation that create a unique landscape. Kewaskum is located at the southern end of the northern unit of the Kettle Moraine, so lays claim to being a gateway to the forest, although at 30,000 acres it is so huge that there are many towns that lead into it from different directions.

A Wisconsin farm boy turned writer, Glenway Wescott was born in Kewaskum in 1901. His career spanned several decades. He was best known for his novella *The Pilgrim Hawk* and two of his novels, *The Grandmothers* and *Apartment in Athens*. After *Apartment in Athens*, he never wrote another novel, though he continued to write other works and lived for another 42 years. Aside from his novels, he published two books of poetry, four collections of short stories, a couple books of essays, and his journals were published posthumously. Wescott was an expatriate who lived in Germany, England, and France. While in France he associated with other writers like Gertrude Stein, Jean Cocteau, and Ernest Hemingway. He was openly gay in the early 1900s, which at that time could be a dangerous thing (though it's getting more dangerous again in the early 2002's). Wescott started a relationship with his life partner, Monroe Wheeler, in 1919 and while it was not monogamous their relationship lasted until his death in 1987. The city doesn't do much to claim him.

KEWAUNEE: Home of the World's Largest Grandfather Clock

At 35 feet, ten inches tall, Kewaunee's grandfather clock bills itself as the World's Largest Grandfather clock. Appropriately for such a tall clock it is made out of redwood. It is a colonial style working clock with three faces. The clock was suggested by Robert Kohrt of Svoboda Industries as a gift to the city for America's bicentennial in 1976. It was built by a crew led by Jake and Rodney Schleis. The clock has been moved several times, starting at the Svoboda plant. From there, it was moved to the Top of the Hill shop in 1984 and stayed there until the business was closed and the building sold. Since 2014 it has been located at the trailhead of the Ahnapee State Trail. After it was moved to its present location workers spent a year working on maintenance and cleaning of it. Its power was restarted in 2015 and the chimes now continue to ring every quarter hour. There is no charge to view or photograph the clock.

L

LA CROSSE: Home of the World's Largest Six-Pack

Wisconsin has a reputation for its drinking culture and also claims a fair number of the "world's largest," including the World's Largest Six-Pack of beer in La Crosse. At the former Heileman's Brewery there are six round storage containers towering over 50 feet tall each. A sign at the base of them relates that the storage tanks can hold 22,200 barrels of beer, which would fill over seven million cans and would be a six-pack a day for 3,351 years for just one individual. A year after they were erected, they were painted to look like Heileman's signature beer brand, Old Style. After the brewery was sold in 1999 the new owners painted over the beer cans with plain white paint. Several years later they redecorated the containers with their own brand of beer, La Crosse Lager, making them the largest six-pack in the world again.

LAKE GENEVA: Newport of the West
                 Birthplace of Dungeons and Dragons
                 Home of the Only Mail Boat Jumpers in the
United States

Newport, Rhode Island is well-known as a resort town and is famous for its many mansions. Situated within a short trip from Providence, Boston, and New York, many of the wealthiest families in the country built mansions and large summer cottages in the city, including the Astors and Vanderbilts. Lake Geneva gained the name Newport of the West because it also developed into a resort town on water. Likewise, it became a destination for a large number of wealthy families who built mansions there, mostly from the Chicago area. This included names like Schwinn and Wrigley. In later years Lake Geneva would see names like Al Capone and later Hugh Hefner, who built the first of his Playboy mansions in the city (now the Grand Geneva Resort).

In addition to the opulent mansions, Lake Geneva was the birthplace of the role-playing game Dungeons and Dragons. Designed by Gary Gygax and Dave Arneson the game was released in 1974, published by their company, TSR. Despite conservative fears of Satanic influences on the players of the game it became hugely popular and is still played by millions of people around the world. There has been no evidence of players converting to Satanism or descending into hell as a result of the game. The Dungeon Hobby Shop Museum is located in the former headquarters of TSR and displays D & D memorabilia and collectibles. It is a hobby shop as well. The museum is open by appointment only. Also in Lake Geneva is the Birthplace of DND, the Gygax house where the game was developed. The house can now be rented for up to ten players for ten hours to play the game at the place where it was created, a unique experience for lovers of the game. On Wrigley Drive there is a memorial stone tablet honoring Dungeons and Dragons embedded in the bricks leading up to the entrance of the Riviera Center. Funds are being raised to erect a statue in honor of Gary Gygax. The design will have him seated at the head of a table with an original Dungeons and Dragons map atop the table, allowing fans to play the game right at the memorial.

Back in the early 1900s, there were no roads around Lake Geneva, so many of the wealthy mansion owners had boats in order to get from one place to another. Starting in 1916 a mailboat was used to deliver mail to the homes around the lake and the tradition continues to this day. Mail is sorted by the carrier on the boat and then delivered to dozens of homes each day. In addition to delivering the mail, the boat carries passengers who get to watch teenagers perform their summer jobs by jumping from the front of the boat onto the piers of houses around Lake Geneva. After jumping, they race up the pier, quickly drop off the mail, and then run back and leap onto the back of the boat, which never stops moving. Occasionally the jumpers slip and fall into the water and the boat has to go back to pick them up.

LAKE MILLS: City of the Pyramids

There have been reports for years of supposed man-made structures that look like pyramids at the bottom of Rock Lake next to Lake Mills. In the 1930s divers reported seeing pyramidal structures and some animal effigies in the lake. In 1937 scuba diver Max Nohl investigated and reported back that from the lake bottom the structure he found was 29 feet high. The maximum depth of the lake is 60 feet. Nohl also said that by putting his hand in the ooze at the bottom it was clear that it continued further down. Some people believe Native American cultures built the pyramids before the lake filled in with water. Some believe there is alien activity at the lake or that it might be the lost city of Atlantis. Others believe it is Solomon's Temple (maybe transported there by the aliens?). Still others dismiss the theories and say that the pyramids are likely natural formations from glaciation. Despite all the reports, dive teams from the state have not been able to find anything proving the existence of pyramids in the lake. In the early 1960s a dive team from the Milwaukee Public Museum arrived at the conclusion of rock piles from glaciers. No clear photos or concrete evidence of the pyramids has ever surfaced. However, that hasn't stopped the local Chamber of Commerce from promoting the idea of pyramids in the lake to potential tourists.

LAKE NEBAGAMON: Home of the World's Heaviest Ball of Twine

While cities in Minnesota and Kansas both claim to be the home of the world's largest ball of twine, a man in Lake Nebagamon claimed to have created the World's Heaviest Ball of Twine. It weighs about 6,000 pounds more than the ones in either of the other states, which is why it is billed as the World's *Heaviest* Ball of Twine rather than the largest. The man who created it was James Kotera, who started wrapping it in 1979 and continued whenever possible until he passed away in early 2023. He had also created Junior, a smaller ball made of string. After his passing a fundraising effort was started to move the ball of twine from Kotera's house to City Hall.

LAKE TOMAHAWK: World's Capital of Snowshoe Baseball

Perhaps it's the snowshoe baseball capital of the world because no one else plays it. But in Lake Tomahawk, they do. Well, actually they don't—it's softball. And despite the wooden snowshoes, it's played in the summer. The players do wear snowshoes, roam the outfield, and run around the bases on a field covered with about ten inches of sawdust to simulate snowshoeing. The home team is called the Snowhawks and they play against teams made up of police and fire department personnel, the local news teams, bars, and others. The games are held every Monday from the third week in June until the end of August at Snowshoe Park. There is a July 4th game every year. The games are always free to attend, but a butterfly net is passed around for donations. Food, including dozens of homemade pies in a wide variety of flavors, is always available. The games were originally played on the ice in the 1940s and 1950s and eventually shifted away from winter. Snowshoe baseball in the summer has been a regular event in Lake Tomahawk since it was started by Town Chairman Ray Sloan in 1961.

LAONA: Home of the World's Largest Soup Kettle

In the heart of Laona the world's largest soup kettle is on display, held up by a large wooden tripod. It is three feet deep with a circumference of seven feet. Years ago, it was used once a year to cook soup for the community. One day in August, the John Russell family would invite everyone in the community to come to their cabin and enjoy some homemade soup made in the large kettle. The Russells hosted the event for 30 years starting in 1919 and served hundreds of people. The annual Community Soup eventually grew so large it was taken over by the local Lions Club in 1950. The Community Soup is still held every year and is a big gathering. However, the giant kettle is no longer used to cook the soup and residents have to bring their own bowls.

LEON: Home of Gatorfest

As travelers enter the small Monroe County town of Leon, they are greeted by a sign announcing the dates of the annual Leon Gatorfest. A couple of businesses along the street have alligators painted on their signs. It strikes one as rather odd. Most people might stop and think to themselves, "This is Wisconsin, not Florida. There are cows here, not alligators." And they would be right, but *USA Today* didn't know that when they wrote a story back in 2002 about pet alligators on the loose in places far-flung from Florida. They included details about a pet alligator on the loose in the town of Leon. Someone from the community wrote to advise the newspaper that there were no alligators in the town and no issues with an escaped pet alligator. When the paper responded that it was definitely Leon, Wisconsin, not another state, the citizens decided if *USA Today* insisted they had alligators, they would hold a Gatorfest to celebrate it. The festival has taken place every August since then with food stands, music, a stand-still parade, reptile exhibit, and surprisingly, no escaped alligators.

LODI: Home of Susie the Duck

Back in the 1940s a mallard hen found a concrete basket in Veterans' Park in downtown Lodi and decided it would be a good place to nest. She laid eggs and citizens of the town became enthralled with her. Many people would stop by regularly, excitedly waiting for the eggs to hatch and then watching the little ducklings as they began to grow. The mallard came back for many years, raising a couple broods a year. In 1948 Susie officially became the city's mascot and at the time she became a national news story. After the original Susie, many other ducks found the same basket and also made it their nesting place. Townspeople called each one Susie in honor of the first mallard matriarch. Every year in August the city celebrates Susie the Duck Day. In addition to the usual festival standards like food, races, and parades, the big highlight of Susie the Duck Day is the annual rubber duck race held on Spring Creek. Somewhere over 1,500 rubber ducks are dropped into the creek and people can buy tickets and win prizes depending on how their duck finishes the race.

LONE ROCK: Coldest Spot in the Nation

Lone Rock was indeed the coldest spot in the nation on January 30, 1951, when the temperature dropped to an official -53 degrees. It may have been even colder, but the thermometer at Tri-County Airport wasn't working well due to the extreme cold. The man who recorded the official temperatures at the airport, Ben Silko, found the mercury had dropped into the bulb of the thermometer, which was accurate to -47 degrees. Because it was below the -47 mark, he had to calibrate up from that mark to the top of the bulb to get the official reading, which he felt was likely even lower than the official -53 degrees he recorded. The sign at the entrance to the town which is maintained by the village says, "We are the Coldest in the Nation . . . with the Warmest Heart," with a polar bear atop a heart with the words, "Welcome to Lone Rock." While it's no longer the lowest official temperature in Wisconsin history, it is just a couple of degrees off of the record. The official lowest was set many years after Lone Rock's cold day and stands at -55 at Couderay in 1996.

LONG LAKE: Walleye Capital of Wisconsin

Less lofty than Presque Isle, which bills itself as the Walleye Capital of the World, Long Lake claims to be the Walleye Capital of Wisconsin. But it is not a town with a sign at its border. It is a lake that stakes the claim. Long Lake is located in Washburn County and is almost 3,500 acres, 19 miles long (thus the name), and has spots as much as 74 feet deep. It is known for its great fishing, and provides a particularly good habitat for walleye. Many other fish species such as pike, bass, and panfish can be taken on the lake, but walleye is the one that fishers go there to catch. There are four boat landings, several bait shops and restaurants, and other attractions around the lake.

M

MADISON: State Capital

The one definitely uncontested capital in Wisconsin is the state capital, which has always been Madison. Prior to statehood, Belmont was the first territorial capital in 1836 and legislators there voted to make Madison the capital city. At the time it was mostly marshland on the isthmus and legislators didn't even meet in the city until 1838. Between Belmont and Madison people may be surprised to find that present-day Burlington, Iowa was the second territorial capital in 1837, followed by Madison a year later. When Wisconsin became a state in 1848 Madison became the first and only state capital. The Legislature met in the first Capitol building in Madison for the first time in 1838 while Wisconsin was still a territory. The building continued to be used upon statehood. That building was replaced in 1863 and the second building remained the Capitol until it burned down in 1904. Construction on the current Capitol was begun in 1906 and completed in 1917. It houses the Supreme Court, Governor's office, and Legislature and has served the state for more than a century.

MANAWA: Rodeo City

Wisconsin is definitely not the Old West, but there are a

surprising number of line dancers, pickup trucks, horses, cowboy hats and boots, and rodeos all around the state. In Manawa, rodeo is big-time. Called "The Greatest Show on Dirt," Manawa is home to the Mid-Western Rodeo, held annually around the Independence Day weekend. The rodeo was selected as the Great Lakes Circuit Medium Rodeo of the Year 12 times between 2007 and 2023. The event is sponsored by the local Lions Club which donates proceeds to community organizations and projects. It started in 1959 after a local resident saw an ad for a rodeo and suggested to the Lions that it might be a good fundraising event for the town. The proof was provided when the first one drew about 7,000 attendees. These days the rodeo draws contestants from throughout the Midwest and about 15,000 fans every year.

MANITOWOC: Maritime Capital of Wisconsin
                        Sputnik Crash Site

When thinking of shipbuilding one does not necessarily think of Wisconsin right away. Yet Manitowoc lays a claim as the Shipbuilding Capital of Wisconsin. The city is on the shore of Lake Michigan and was one of the largest inland shipbuilding ports in the United States through much of the 20th century. Manitowoc Shipbuilding started building commercial vessels in 1902 and continued shipbuilding until it closed in 1972. Hundreds of different kinds of ships were built there, from freighters to car ferries. During World War I, 30 all-steel ships were built for the Navy and during World War II the city's shipbuilders built 28 submarines to assist the war effort, four of which were lost in action. Burger Boat Company still continues building custom yachts in Manitowoc. Due to the city's history of creating so many vessels, Wisconsin's largest maritime museum is located in Manitowoc. The Wisconsin Maritime Museum has displays celebrating all of the state's maritime history and even has a real submarine that is available to tour. Surprisingly, the Cobia is not one of the submarines built in Manitowoc. In addition to all of the other maritime history in the city, the last coal-fired passenger steamship in operation in the country, the S. S. Badger, is a car ferry that arrives and departs at Manitowoc and travels across Lake Michigan to Ludington, Michigan once a day in season. It has been plying the waters of Lake Michigan since 1953.

On September 6, 1962, the only known surviving piece of Russia's Sputnik IV, which had launched more than two years earlier, crashed to earth in the middle of Eighth Street in front of Manitowoc's art museum. It was a 20-pound remnant that embedded itself in the asphalt of the street and was discovered by a pair of police officers during their morning patrol. The piece was studied and eventually returned to Russia due to international agreements. The site where it landed was marked with a brass ring. Every September the Rahr West Art Museum hosts Sputnikfest to commemorate the event. Highlights are the wacky costumes attendees are encouraged to wear and a Miss Space Debris Pageant.

MARATHON COUNTY: Ginseng Capital of the World

One of the few counties to proclaim itself a capital, Marathon County is the state's largest producer and exporter of ginseng, a highly sought and prized root in Asia. Almost all of Wisconsin's ginseng is produced in the county and most of that is exported to China for use in herbal medicines. In Wisconsin ginseng was historically used by Native Americans for medicinal purposes. In China and elsewhere, it is prized as an aphrodisiac. Wild ginseng was traded in Marathon County as early as the late 1800s. One of the first in the area to cultivate ginseng was John Koehler, who created the first ginseng farm in the county in 1901. Farm production of the crop took off after 1904 when four young brothers—Edward, Henry, John, and Walter Fromm—decided to cultivate the plant. They developed many of the practices still used by ginseng farmers today, including how to shade the plants, which is done with wood laths or with dark cloth. The Fromm brothers farm in Hamburg is considered to be where the trade really started to develop and is on the National Register of Historic Places. Wisconsin ginseng from the area is now considered among the best in the world and well over 90% of U. S. exports of it are from the area. Nearly 200 growers in the state create millions of dollars in exports every year. And because Wisconsin loves its festivals, the International Wisconsin Ginseng Festival was started in Marathon's county seat, Wausau, in 2017 as a way to celebrate the root, raise awareness, and increase exports.

MARINETTE COUNTY: Waterfalls Capital of Wisconsin

Another county claim is from Marinette. There is something magical about waterfalls that draws people to them. The sound of rushing water, the sight of water continuously cascading over a rock face into a pool or river below appeals to our senses in some elemental way. Having a number of them within close proximity makes that elemental yearning easy to satisfy. Fifteen waterfalls in Marinette County allow it to stake a claim as the Waterfalls Capital of Wisconsin. It is even inscribed on the county's official seal. With names like Four Foot Falls, Eight Foot Falls, Twelve Foot Falls, and Eighteen Foot Falls tourists should pretty much know what they are getting at those. There are larger falls such as Long Slide Falls, at which the water drops over about 50 feet of good-sized rock formations. There are also falls with picturesque names like Horseshoe Falls, Quiver Falls, and Piers Gorge. There is even a city in the county named Niagara, which is home to Little Quinnesec Falls. Most of the waterfalls in the county have easy access trails to get to them and many have viewing areas and bridges from which to get good views or pictures of them.

MARSHFIELD: Home of the World's Largest Round Barn
Home of Jurustic Park

There are many round barns scattered throughout the state of Wisconsin, including the World's Largest Round Barn, which is located in Marshfield. Construction of the barn began in 1915 on the Wood County fairgrounds and it was completed in 1916. It has a diameter of 150 feet and a height of 70 feet and was built and is still used as a show barn for the fair. Other uses over the years include barn dances, shows, church services, and more. It can be rented as an event space and tours are provided.

Jurustic Park is another of Wisconsin's folk-art sites, a sculpture park loaded with metal creatures from the mind and hands of artist Clyde Wynia, who quips that all of them are from the Iron Age. Wynia claims that he has recreated extinct animals from the nearby McMillian Marsh. Visitors might come across dragons, giant turtles, and numerous other whimsical creatures at the park. Wynia started building sculptures on the site just a few miles outside of Marshfield about 30 years ago and now 15,000 or more visitors stop by every year. More than half a dozen additional figures by the artist are located on the streets of Marshfield.

MERCER: Loon Capital of the World

This capital title refers to the bird, of which there are many in northern Wisconsin, although the long-time head of the Wisconsin branch of the Ku Klux Klan also hailed from Mercer. Besides having a large natural population of loons, Mercer also has the world's largest talking loon, a huge fiberglass creature named Claire d' Loon that actually speaks, though in bird, not in any human language. She's 16 feet high and weighs 2,000 pounds. The town is the Loon Capital of the World because of the real birds and Claire was put in place at the Chamber of Commerce in 1981 to honor the striking waterfowl with the beautiful, haunting call. According to the Mercer Chamber of Commerce, the town has the "highest concentration of nesting loon pairs in the continental United States." There are more than 100 lakes in the immediate area and visitors can find loons on pretty much any of them. Except for the largest lakes, you can generally only find one mating pair on each lake. They often dive into the water and reappear many yards away as they are capable of diving as much as 200 feet and can stay under the water for up to ten minutes. The town hosts an annual Loon Day with food, a street dance, and a loon calling contest.

MERRIMAC: Home of the Merrimac Free Ferry

The Merrimac ferry, currently the Colsac III, is the only free ferry in the Midwest. It crosses Lake Wisconsin, which is part of the Wisconsin River, between Columbia and Sauk counties (thus Colsac). Though usually called the Merrimac ferry, it serves both Merrimac and Okee on the two sides of the river. Colsac III carries cars, motorcycles, bicycles, and pedestrians on a seven-minute trip when there is no ice on the lake. Once it opens for the season it operates 24 hours a day every day of the week. It typically carries 200,000 to 300,000 a year. Ferry service at the location started in the 1840s. The first ferry at the site was literally pulled across the river, some say by the ferry operators and others that it was by horses. It was replaced by a gas-powered ferry in 1900, then replaced by the first Colsac in 1924, which carried eight vehicles. The Colsac II held 12 cars. The current ferry holds up to 15 cars a trip and is still pulled across the river, but by cables in the water. Because of the limited number of vehicles the ferry can take at one time, concession stands are available on shore for those waiting for the next round. Some people go just for the ice cream and to watch the ferry and don't bother crossing. The State of Wisconsin took over operation of the ferry in 1933 and it has been free since that time. The state and federal government have occasionally considered replacing the ferry with a bridge, but it has continued to operate and has outlasted about 500 other ferries that existed in Wisconsin but have ceased operation.

MIDDLETON: Home of the Mustard Museum

Originally opened as the Mount Horeb Mustard Museum, the National Mustard Museum moved to its current location in Middleton when it outgrew its original space. It was started by attorney Barry Levenson with his own small mustard collection and has grown to well over 6,000 mustards from every state and dozens of countries. In addition to the mustards there are collectibles and mustard exhibits, as well as a gift shop. Highlights of the museum include videos on mustard at "Mustard Piece Theatre," recipes from Mrs. Mustard's Kitchen, Poupon U, and a quiz game. Free samples are available in the store. Group tours are available. The museum has been featured on numerous television and radio shows and in several national publications. It is free and is open every day of the week all year long, with the exception of a few holidays. Because of the museum, Middleton now celebrates National Mustard Day on the first Saturday in August. With a flair for self-promotion, the holiday was created by the museum. Middleton also hosts a Worldwide Mustard Competition, which features several hundred entries from around the world.

MILWAUKEE: Beer Capital of the World
             The Most German City in America
             The City of Festivals
             Childhood Home of Golda Meier

Milwaukee's biggest claim to fame is undoubtedly its beer. It is Famous for Beer, Brew City, and the Beer Capital of the World. The professional baseball team is the Brewers in honor of the city's beer history. Milwaukee's first brewery opened in 1840 by Welsh immigrants before Wisconsin was even a state. There were 30 breweries started within a 20-year span after that. Among many smaller breweries, some of the larger and best known were Best (which became Pabst), Blatz, Gettelman, Miller, and Schlitz. There are still several large breweries in the city, and a good number of small craft beer producers. Many of Milwaukee's breweries were founded by German immigrants who introduced German-style lager, which became the predominant type of beer produced in the city. Most of the founders either had brewery businesses in Germany which they moved to Wisconsin, or they had experience in the industry back home.

Milwaukee is associated with beer, brats, and Germans. The beer barons were not the only Germans to immigrate to Milwaukee. By 1860 more than a third of the city's population consisted of native Germans. German immigrants settled all over the state and Milwaukee was particularly attractive. It became known as the German Athens of North America. While Athens was considered the center of ancient culture, Milwaukee was considered the cultural center of Germans in America. Today, there are still German restaurants, beer gardens, German speakers, about 30 German American societies, an Octoberfest celebration, and the largest German festival in the world.

Milwaukee loves all of its festivals. Throughout the summer there are large festivals along the waterfront at Henry Maier Festival Park, which draw thousands of people to the site. The major summer festivals include PrideFest Milwaukee, Polish Fest, SummerFest (billed as the world's largest music festival and held over three weekends), Festa Italiana, German Fest, Black Arts Fest, Irish Fest, Mexican Fiesta, Labor Fest, and Pet Fest. The park also hosts many other smaller festivals. Throughout the year there are many church, neighborhood, and other festivals at the Summerfest grounds and throughout the city. Among them are Weird Fest, Winterfest, the Jazz Heritage Festival, International Anime Music Festival, Milwaukee Blues Festival, Lakefront Festival of Art, Homegrown Music Festival, Croatian Fest, Armenian Fest, Milwaukee Brewfest,

Octoberfest, Jewish Food Festival, and dozens of others.

Milwaukee was the childhood home of Golda Meir. Born in Kyiv her family moved to Milwaukee to escape pogroms in their homeland. She attended Fourth Street Grade School (now the Golda Meier School for Gifted and Talented Youth) and North Division High School in Milwaukee. Although she lived with her sister in Denver for a brief period as a teenager, she moved back to Milwaukee in time to graduate from North Division. She became a Zionist as a youth and after marriage she and her husband moved to Palestine where she became involved in politics. After the creation of Israel in 1948 Meir became the country's labor minister, foreign minister, served in the Knesset, and later, became the Prime Minister from 1969 to 1974. She was only the third female Prime Minister of any country in history.

MINERAL POINT: Where Wisconsin Began
                                   Hometown of Alan Ludden

Mineral Point is considered Where Wisconsin Began because of the history of the place. It is thought to be the third-oldest city in the state, though others claim that distinction, too. While Green Bay and Prairie du Chien are older, the real settlement of the state by frontiersmen began in earnest in the 1820s with the lead rush in southwestern Wisconsin. Miners flocked to the lead mining region to make their fortunes and settled in places like Mineral Point, Shullsburg, Hazel Green, Platteville, and others. That population boom led the area to become the political center of the territory, with the first territorial legislative session being held in nearby Belmont, and many of the residents of the area becoming the earliest movers and shakers in government and business circles. The first territorial governor, Henry Dodge, was sworn into office in the town. The early miners who settled in the Mineral Point area were expert miners from Cornwall, England and their influence remains in the stone cottages all over the town and in pasties, a meat pie that miners' wives made for their men down in the mines.

Mineral Point is the hometown of Alan Ludden, best known as the host of the long-running television game show, "Password," which aired in different versions for about 20 years. He also hosted "College Bowl" and several other shows. Ludden was the long-time husband of television star Betty White, whom he met as a celebrity guest panelist on the set of "Password." Even though his family moved to several other Wisconsin cities and then to Texas when he was nine, he is buried at Graceland Cemetery in Mineral Point.

MINOCQUA: The Island City

No man is an island, but some towns are. The trademarked name of The Island City comes from the fact that the city center of Minocqua, a popular tourist destination in northern Wisconsin, was built on an island when it was first created. Most of the important civic buildings such as the police station, Campanille Center for the Arts, and Minocqua Center, which houses city offices and the library, are located there. Looking at local business and organization names it seems like half or more are named Island City, followed by the type of business.

MONICO: Home of the World's Largest Mechanical Globe Planetarium
              Home of the Rhinelapus

The Kovac Planetarium took ten years to build and was constructed mostly by one man, Frank Kovac, in his back yard. Interested in the night sky at an early age, the planetarium was the culmination of a dream and a lot of hard work for Kovac. It was built during his off-hours from his day job at a paper mill and with only a high school education. Kovac hand-painted more than 5,000 stars in the planetarium. When it was done his handiwork became the World's Largest Mechanical Planetarium. It is only the fourth one built since the 16th century and one of only three now in existence. The distinction is that it is mechanically operated and the globe revolves around the audience, so the stars literally move past them. Most planetariums project the stars onto the interior of the building and the projections appear to move across the night sky. Kovac's globe weighs two tons and has a 22-foot diameter. It is on a 45-degree angle to match the stars' positions relative to Monico's location in northern Wisconsin. It seats a couple dozen people at a time and Kovac is the host of the show.

The Rhinelapus is a green monster on display in a shelter at the

Monico Community Park. The beast was originally part of a white pine, but was thought to look like a genetic mutation of a rhinoceros, elephant, and octopus. The man who found it, Guy Dailey, had it hauled to his tavern where he put it on display and named it the Rhinelapus. It was later painted and came to be known by locals as the Green Monster. A later owner of the Lake Venus Tavern did not want to keep it and told one of the residents of Monico that it would be gone forever if they didn't take it off of his hands. The Green Monster had become so beloved by the town's residents that people banded together to save it and move it to a safe space in the city park where future generations would also be able to enjoy it, or maybe be petrified by it.

MONROE: Swiss Cheese Capital of the U.S.A

Depending on who you speak to, Monroe is known as the Swiss Cheese Capital of the U.S.A, the Cheese Capital of the U.S.A., Gateway to Cheese Country, Cheese City, or Swiss Cheese Capital of the World. One might be inclined to think that the Swiss Cheese Capital of the World would be somewhere in Switzerland, but Monroe believes it has a claim to the title. The key word in all of these is cheese, and due to the large influx of Swiss immigrants in the 1800s Swiss cheese took prominence in Monroe and Green County. Area cheese factories produce more than four dozen varieties of cheese and the city is the only place in America where limburger cheese is made, but the claim is about Swiss cheese, which is king in the city. Monroe hosts Cheese Days every other year (the even years), a large celebration of cheese and its importance to the city, county, and state. It started in 1914 and is said to be the oldest food festival in the Midwest. Monroe is also home to the National Historic Cheesemaking Center Museum, where you can learn about the history of cheese and visit an old-fashioned one kettle cheese factory that was left intact in 1917 and later moved to the museum as a display. Once a year, on the second Saturday of June (remember, June is Dairy Month), visitors can watch a 90-pound wheel of Swiss cheese being made the old-fashioned way.

MONTFORT: Home of the Fort

Though historical details are sketchy there was supposedly a fort built on a small hill just a little east of Montfort for the protection of the mining settlers and their families during the Black Hawk War in the 1830s. That is where the town got its name, from the French word "mont" for mountain and the word "fort." Of course, there are no mountains in Wisconsin—just hills—and the fort no longer exists, and nobody knows the exact location where it once stood. The town's movie theater was called The Fort Theatre, but it hasn't shown a film since it was closed in 1961. With a current population of a little over 700, the village, unlike the fort, does still exist and its citizens do their best to remember its heritage despite the long-lost fort.

MOSINEE: Site of a Communist Takeover

Not in the tourist brochures or mentioned on the city website, Mosinee hosted a mock Communist takeover of the city on May 1, 1950, timed to coincide with International Workers' Day. It was a paranoid response to the supposed Red Scare of the 1950s. It was announced to the press in advance, perhaps to make sure residents knew what was happening and to ensure press coverage of the event. The advance notice gave Communist sympathizers a chance to distribute leaflets the night before decrying the event as capitalist propaganda. Sponsored by the American Legion, the town newspaper was renamed *Red Star* and proclaimed that Communists had taken over the city. The paper included instructions to the citizens of the community. Legionnaires in costumes demanded to see papers, created permits for citizens for almost everything they might do, including coming and going past the town's border. Men with guns arrested the mayor and police chief, imprisoned religious and other town leaders, and searched homes for American and capitalist propaganda. Prices for consumer goods skyrocketed in one day, soup lines formed, and flags and other symbols of Communism were seen around the town. Heavily covered in the press at the time, the entire day was created as a warning to America about the dangers of Communism. At the end of the day the charade ended and citizens burned all the red propaganda, raised the American flag again, and sang "God Bless America" as one, thankful to live in Mosinee in the land of the free rather than the totalitarian state they created to show how bad it could be.

MOUNT HOREB: Troll Capital of the World

Trolls are beings from Norse mythology who live in caves or other places underground, sometimes depicted as giants, but usually more the size of little people. In America, they are generally thought of as living under bridges due to an early English translation of the Norwegian story, "Three Billy Goats Gruff." Mount Horeb's heritage is heavily Norwegian. In 1900 about 75% of the population was comprised of Norwegian immigrants, so Norwegian pride, culture, and mythology permeate the town to this day. One can see Norwegian flags, businesses with Scandinavian names, signs in Norwegian such as "Velkommen" (Norwegian for "welcome"), and trolls. What started in the 1970s with a few imported wooden trolls placed outside a Scandinavian gift shop, Open House Imports, has turned into what is called the Trollway, with trolls lined up along the main thoroughfare through town. In Mount Horeb, trolls don't live in caves or under bridges; they are proudly displayed out in the open. The reason for this is that in the 1980s a bypass was built around Mount Horeb and city officials feared travelers would also bypass the town. They asked local woodcarver, Michael Feeney, to carve trolls as a way to possibly attract passing motorists to get off the highway and visit the town. Over the years, other woodcarvers have added their creations. Most are placed outside of local businesses, but some are scattered elsewhere around the city. There are at least two dozen in all. An official living troll called Jorgen appears at local events, further cementing the troll title.

MUSCODA: Morel Mushroom Capital of Wisconsin

Morel mushrooms are a type of mushroom sought by chefs for their unique and delicious flavor. They have been difficult to cultivate and wild morels can only be found for a few weeks each year, and under certain conditions, so morel hunting in the spring is both an adventure and a potential profitmaking venture. The area's woods are fertile ground for the sought-after mushroom. For many, finding enough to fill a bag for use in their own kitchens is all the satisfaction they need. For others, the idea of cashing in on their finds is what drives them, though they probably keep some for themselves, too. The village of Muscoda hosts an annual Morel Mushroom Festival every year in the spring, always the weekend after Mother's Day, with all the standards—a parade, food, music, and more. Mushroom brats are available at Mushroom Headquarters and morel hunters can sell their finds at the festival. When available, visitors can enjoy fried morel mushrooms.

NECEDAH: Home of the Necedah Shrine

The Necedah Shrine, officially the Queen of the Holy Rosary/Mediatrix of Peace Shrine, was created due to the claims of visions reported by farmwife Mary Ann Van Hoof, who said the Virgin Mary came to her in November of 1949. She reported eight more visions over the course of the next year and many more times over a 34-year span, not only from Mary, but also from several saints and even Jesus. One hundred thousand pilgrims were there for one of the visions in August of 1950. Dismissed by the Catholic Church, Van Hoof continued to claim the visions were real and eventually broke away from the Church over their refusal to acknowledge what she claimed to have seen. She told followers that the Virgin wanted to lead people to the truth through the rosary, and appeared especially for the youth. As time went on, the visions included political aspects against Communism. She also claimed Mary told her that she helped Washington win the Revolutionary War and Abe Lincoln win the Civil War. Because of this, the Shrine grounds are a strange combination of religious and patriotic displays, built according to instructions given to her in the visions. The shrine is free and open to the public.

NEILLSVILLE: Home of Chatty Belle, the World's Largest Talking Cow

Does more really need to be said? If so, Chatty Belle might say it. Chatty Belle originated as an exhibit at the 1964 World's Fair in

New York and now resides in Neillsville, next to the Wisconsin pavilion from that same World's Fair. She used to have the company of the world's largest cheese replica and a smaller Holstein, Bullet, who was her son. She is 16 feet tall and 20 feet long. She's not a great conversationalist as she mostly lectures visitors about Wisconsin's famed dairy industry. She was brought to Neillsville by Central Wisconsin Broadcasting, which owned the local radio station. They held a contest to name the cow, which was won by a first grader from Loyal, Wisconsin. The child won 100 pounds of butter as the prize. It's likely she may have preferred to win a Barbie doll or a bicycle or something else, but Wisconsin butter is what she got. There have been times when Chatty Belle was silenced, but these days she speaks a lot more, with special messages recorded for holidays in addition to her dairy spiel. Keeping up with the times, she has discovered social media and has her own Facebook page and Twitter account.

NEW GLARUS: America's Little Switzerland

Founded by settlers from Glarus, Switzerland, New Glarus retains its personality as a small Swiss village in the heart of America. Long after the first 108 Swiss settlers arrived in 1845 there are moments when being in New Glarus feels like traveling in another country. There are countless businesses housed in chalets, Swiss flags everywhere, a Wilhelm Tell Festival to celebrate Switzerland's best known folk hero, the Alpine Festival, a Heidi Pageant, October Fest, Polka Fest, and Volksfest, which is a celebration of Swiss independence sponsored by the Maennerchor, a European-style men's singing group. There is even a yodeling club, something not found in every American city. The club has members who not only yodel, but play the alpenhorn at most of the events listed above. The Chamber of Commerce website is swisstown.com. Those who want to know what it was like when the original settlers came can visit the Swiss Historical Village, a recreation of an 1850 Swiss settlement. There are more than a dozen buildings reflecting the life of the times, including a blacksmith shop, school, cabin, and several others. Some of the buildings are original and some are replicas. New Glarus is home of the Swiss Center of North America, which is dedicated to preserving the history of the Swiss emigration story and Swiss culture.

NEW HOLSTEIN: Cowtown, U. S. A.

New Holstein was not named after the cow, but after the Schleswig-Holstein area of Germany after 70 immigrants from there arrived in the area and settled. Forty years later virtually all of its inhabitants were still German or descended from German settlers. Holsteins are the black and white cows that are seen in fields throughout the Badger state. They are considered the highest producing dairy cows. New Holstein has taken advantage of that connection by calling themselves Cowtown, U. S. A. While there is no sign proclaiming this and it is not on the city or Chamber of Commerce websites, there has been a Cowtown Craft Festival and at least one business with the name Cowtown in it. Locals remember it and may still use it, but the nickname has fallen out of use over the last number of years.

NEW LONDON: Birthplace of the American Water Spaniel

One of only five breeds of dog developed in the United States and recognized as distinct breeds, the American water spaniel is the only one from Wisconsin. Dr. F. J. Pfeifer of New London worked to perfect and standardize the breed. Pfeifer, John Scofield, Thomas Brogdan, and the American Water Spaniel Club were responsible for much of the work of obtaining recognition by the American Kennel Club (AKC), the premiere organization in the United States devoted to purebred dogs. Recognition by the AKC came in 1940. Previous recognition had been granted by the United Kennel Club in 1920 and the Field Dog Stud Book in 1938. The doctor's own dog, Curly Pfeifer, was the first registered dog of the breed. The American water spaniel is a hunting dog known to be versatile on both land and water. It is good at retrieving waterfowl, but also works well with flushing prey on land. It became the state dog in 1986 after five years of lobbying work by eighth graders from New London. The American Water Spaniel Club named the New London Public Museum as the place to archive its documents, which can be viewed by appointment.

NORTH FREEDOM: Home of the Mid-Continent Railway Museum

The Mid-Continent Railway Museum is a railroading museum that is focused on only a specific period of time, from the Civil War to the end of World War II. It focuses on trains that operated in the upper Midwest and on how trains were the focal point of local communities. The depot and other buildings on the grounds are restorations from the same period. The museum, which started operations in North Freedom in 1963, owns over 100 pieces, including steam locomotive engines, passenger and freight cars, cabooses, and service equipment. Tourists can go on a seven-mile ride on one of the turn-of-the-century trains which passes through the beautiful surrounding countryside. These rides operate throughout the summer, but there is also a fall color ride, a snow train ride, and a Santa Express at other times of the year. The museum has many volunteers, including some whose job is to restore railroad cars.

NORWALK: Black Squirrel Capital of the World
             Gateway to the Tunnels

There is a black squirrel depicted on the sign as you enter Norwalk, and it is easy to see living black squirrels on the streets of the town, which seems to have a preponderance of the rodents compared to other areas of the state. The black squirrel is a genetic variant of the common grey squirrel, with only one in every 10,000 having black fur. The variant is more common in northern areas, but science has yet to explain why more are found in certain parts of northern states, such as Norwalk. Due to having a concentration of the squirrels, the town hosts Black Squirrel Days the second weekend of August every year, with the usual festival fare seen in small towns around the state—food, music, and fireworks, which might just scare the heck out of the little squirrels.

Norwalk's second claim is the Gateway to the Tunnels, a reference to being near the longest tunnel on the Elroy-Sparta Bike Trail, the first rail-to-trail bicycle trail in the United States. The trail is a 32.5-mile-long trail between Sparta and Elroy along an old railroad line with three tunnels along the route. The tunnel near Norwalk is three-quarters of a mile long.

O

OCONTO: Unofficial Walleye Capital of the World
                   Home of America's First Christian Science Church

On the Oconto city, Chamber of Commerce, and tourism websites the authors all proudly note that the city is known for its great fishing, and in Wisconsin that's a big draw. In particular, walleye fishing is noted. The city has been called the Unofficial Walleye Capital of the World, perhaps because another Wisconsin city, Presque Isle, lays claim to being the Walleye Capital of the World. Fishing is available on the Oconto River and on Green Bay, and there are nearly 400 lakes nearby in Oconto County. The harbor has half a dozen boat ramps and a handicap-accessible pier. The city hosts a number of fishing tournaments, including several specifically for walleye: Escape Reality Walleye Open, Master Walleye Circuit, AIM Weekend Walleye Series, and the Sheboygan Walleye Club Battle on the Bay.

The First Church of Christ, Scientist (also known as the Christian Science Church) in Oconto was built in 1886 for $1,137.20. The structure still exists and is mostly in its original state. It is located on Chicago Street and is still used for Christian Science services. It was the first Christian Science church building in the world, not just in the United States. Because of its history, it is listed on the National Register of Historic Places. The religion was founded by Mary Baker Eddy in Boston. The Oconto chapter was started by several local women who had found healing in the teachings of the church. In addition to spiritual healing, Christian Scientists believe that the love Jesus preached can also be a tool to help bring about physical healing. In Oconto, the group of women originally met in the home of one of the members prior to building their church. The building is open to tourists during the summer season.

ONALASKA: Sunfish Capital of the World

Wisconsin seems to have more fish capitals than any other kind. Onalaska's claim is the Sunfish Capital of the World. Along the Great

River Road that runs parallel to the Mississippi River there is a giant fiberglass sunfish, Sunny the Sunfish, welcoming visitors to the city. It is 15 feet high and 25 feet long. The city sits next to 8,300-acre Lake Onalaska, a reservoir of the Mississippi, which holds a good number of pumpkinseed sunfish, as well as bluegill, smallmouth bass, walleye, and other species. There are several ways for fishing aficionados to access the lake, including half a dozen public boat landings and boat launches. The city used to celebrate Sunfish Days, but the event disappeared a number of years ago. Several years after Sunfish Days ended, a new community celebration replaced it to celebrate the city itself, with proceeds helping several community organizations.

OREGON: Horse Capital of Wisconsin

At one time there were supposedly more horses than people in Oregon. There are currently about a dozen and a half stables in the immediate area and a large number of stables within about 30 miles or so of the city. In addition, there are horse breeding, boarding, and training facilities scattered around the countryside and places that offer horseback riding. The Oregon Horse Association promotes horses and riding by holding shows, parades, and educational programs. As a result of all the horse activity in the area, the Chamber of Commerce registered the name Horse Capital of Wisconsin with the Secretary of State's office a number of years ago. While Oregon is still officially the Horse Capital of Wisconsin, the claim has mostly fallen out of use over the last couple of decades.

OSHKOSH: Home of the Experimental Aircraft Association & Fly-In

The Experimental Aircraft Association (EAA) Fly-In attracts close to a million visitors every year and over 10,000 aircraft, making it the world's largest aviation event. The air traffic control tower at Wittman Airport becomes the busiest in the world during the fly-in. The event is officially known as EAA AirVenture Oshkosh. It is a week-long aircraft lover's delight where historic, as well as new and experimental planes, are on display, educational programs are presented, aviation pioneers are in attendance, and visitors are treated to spectacular air shows. For those who can't get enough aircraft history during the week of the fly-in, the EAA Museum is located in Oshkosh and is open year-round. The association was founded in Milwaukee in 1953 with the original purpose of supporting those who built or restored aircraft, but has grown into a group for aviation enthusiasts of all sorts. There are 900 chapters with over 270,000 members worldwide.

OXBO: Wood Tick Capital

Most Wisconsinites (and most people in general) hate wood ticks. Celebrating ticks seems contradictory to our natural instincts. While it doesn't seem like a title that most towns would care to claim, Wood Tick Capital is definitely a distinction, and it is celebrated in an odd way in Oxbo. The town hosts the annual International Wood Tick Race in which a pair of ticks are placed in the center of a circular racetrack and the winner is the tick that gets past the outer edge of the circle first. The loser of each heat gets smashed by a gavel after the heat until only two ticks are left to compete. There are as many as 150 ticks racing every year. For those who don't bring their own ticks and somehow can't find one in northern Wisconsin, there are ticks available for purchase so that everyone who wants to can compete. The entry fee is $1.00 and the winner takes all of the registration money. The last one crawling honors its owner by winning the championship trophy, the monetary award, and title of Wood Tick Racing Champion. And then dies by the gavel just like its vanquished competitors. The race has been held every May at the Oxbo Resort for most of its history, which goes back to the early 1980s.

P

PARDEEVILLE: Home of the U. S. Watermelon Speed Eating and Seed-Spitting Championships

The biggest party in Pardeeville is held every September. Watermelon is the name of the game, or games, at the annual Watermelon Festival. It started with a watermelon seed-spitting contest, but quickly grew as additional contests were added. Contests now include the original seed-spitting contest, watermelon speed eating contest, largest watermelon contest, and watermelon carving contest. There are divisions for men and women, adults, seniors, and youths, and both teams and singles. The winner of the seed-spitting contest is the contestant who spits their seed the farthest within a set of rules that must be followed. For example, seeds are provided; contestants are not allowed to bring their own seeds. The winner of the speed-eating contest is obviously the one in each division who finishes their slice the fastest within the rules. The slice is provided. The winner of the largest watermelon contest is self-evident. The winner of the carving contest is judged by creativity, theme, and presentation. The championships started in 1968.

PARK FALLS: Ruffed Grouse Capital of the World

The ruffed grouse is a sought-after game bird and the most widely distributed one in the United States. Northern Wisconsin is known for large numbers of the bird. Sometimes it is called a drummer because of the way it drums to attract mates and to announce a claim to its territory. The drumming is very loud and is created by the male grouse beating its wings and creating a vacuum. It is usually done from atop a log, but the grouse will step up onto any platform from logs to rocks for its performance. Despite drawing attention to itself with the drumming, the grouse can be difficult to hunt because they are ground birds and blend in well with the underbrush. When they are flushed they take off quickly and it can be hard to even aim let alone get a good shot off before they disappear from view. Surrounded by thousands of acres of grouse-friendly woods, Park Falls laid claim to the ruffed grouse title back in 1985. The state of Wisconsin manages the public lands around the town to ensure quality habitat for the grouse and other animals.

PEPIN: Birthplace of Laura Ingalls Wilder

The Laura Ingalls Wilder History Highway connects sites around the country relating to her life and it starts in Pepin, where she was born and spent the first years of her life. Wilder was the author of the beloved *The Little House on the Prairie* series of children's books. The first book in the series, *Little House in the Big Woods*, was based on living at a cabin in the woods about seven miles north of Pepin.

Some of that land was acquired by locals and a replica cabin was built on the site where the family lived, based on the author's descriptions of it in her first book. The family left Pepin when Wilder was two years old, but came back again two years later and they stayed for another three years, the period that is recounted in the first book. There is a Laura Ingalls Wilder Museum and Gift Store located in Pepin, which houses artifacts from the area and quilts made by Wilder. The city hosts an annual Laura Ingalls Wilder Days the second full weekend of September. The weekend is focused more on the arts and history than the more typical festival events in other towns. It includes crafts, lots of bonnets, and pioneer games. Pepin has a Laura Ingalls Wilder Park, which includes a state historical marker that notes she was born in Pepin and didn't start her writing career until she was 65 years old.

PESHTIGO: Site of the World's Worst-Ever Forest Fire

On the same night as the Great Chicago Fire, another disastrous fire burned in the forests of Wisconsin. In Chicago 300 lives were lost and a large portion of a major American city was destroyed, leaving 100,000 people homeless. Newspapers, and later, historians, wrote a great deal about the Chicago fire. But the fire in Peshtigo destroyed the city and 16 other towns, up to 1.5 million acres of forest in several Wisconsin counties, and claimed about five times as many lives as the Chicago fire, killing more than 1,500 people. Some say as many as 2,500 people may have perished. Most of those lost lives, about 800, were in Peshtigo. The Peshtigo fire remains the deadliest wildfire in American history. Many of the victims, about 350, were buried in a mass grave at the Peshtigo Fire Cemetery as they couldn't be identified. The cemetery is on the National Register of Historic Places and Wisconsin's first historical marker was erected in the cemetery and can be seen there. Some of the population was saved when citizens jumped into the Peshtigo River, but others who jumped in drowned or suffered hypothermia. The city of Peshtigo rebuilt, but other towns destroyed by the fire never did. Today, visitors can honor the dead at the Fire Cemetery. They can learn more about the fire, including stories of tragedy and heroism, at the Peshtigo Fire Museum. The museum houses artifacts that survived the fire, a gift shop, books about the fire, and volunteers who are happy to share their knowledge with visitors. It is located in the first church that was rebuilt after the fire.

PHILLIPS: Home of Fred Smith's Wisconsin Concrete Park
             Trophy White-tail Capital

Featured on national television and known as a celebrated folk artist, Fred Smith created a couple hundred cement sculptures in his back yard in Phillips, Wisconsin. His concrete park has become something of a folk-art shrine. Fred was a retired lumberjack who became a self-taught sculptor. His sculptures, made of concrete, broken glass, and found pieces have garnered him fans and attention around the world. There are 237 sculptures on the site, most of which reflect local history and legend and often show everyday things like a man drinking beer, a wedding party, lumberjacks, and scores of animals. In addition, Smith created sculptures based on American legends and history and a few spiritual pieces. After Smith's death, the site was purchased by the Kohler Foundation in order to save his work. The property later became a county park. There is no admission charge, but donations for maintenance and upkeep are gladly accepted. The city was hit by a bad windstorm in 1977 which necessitated restoration of the site. Another storm hit in 1987 and more restoration had to be done. Experts continuously work to maintain the park in as close of a condition as possible to Smith's original sculptures and vision.

Like much of northern Wisconsin, the woods around Price County, where Phillips is located, are great hunting ground for white-tailed deer. A trophy white-tail has to be at least 160 B&C (Boone and Crockett) points to qualify for trophy status. A point has to be at least one inch in length and the length has to exceed the width to qualify. There are several hunting guide services based in Phillips designed to help hunters get that elusive trophy buck.

PITTSVILLE: Exact Center of Wisconsin

Pittsville was declared the Geographical Center of the State by Governor Walter Kohler, Jr. in 1952. Though it was a ceremonial proclamation, it wasn't just a random proclamation. The claim was first published by the United States Geological Survey in 1923. Land surveyors at the time had determined the exact center of the state to be on a small island in the Yellow River just west of the town. There is a marker at a wayside along the river noting the location. The plaque was donated by the Central Chapter of the Wisconsin Society of Land Surveyors in 1987. There has since been discussion about the methods used to determine the geographical center, including whether the state border extending into Lakes Michigan and Superior were considered by the U. S. Geological Survey, and some who say that with modern technology and computers the center can be pinpointed more accurately. At least until these debates are settled, Pittsville remains the center of the state.

PLAINFIELD: Home of Ed Gein

There is no sign welcoming visitors to the hometown of Ed Gein, and nothing in the town of Plainfield to draw attention to its most infamous citizen. For the most part, citizens of the town would prefer no recognition of their most well-known resident. That's because Ed Gein, behind only Jeffrey Dahmer, is considered the most notorious killer in Wisconsin history. Gein robbed the graves of at least nine people and killed at least two women over the course of a decade, and he is suspected of killing as many as five more. He used the body parts of exhumed remains and from the murders to make lampshades, masks, wastebaskets, bowls, and more. Gein was arrested after killing Bernice Worden in 1957, but he was found legally insane and sent to the Central State Hospital for the Criminally Insane in Waupun. He was later transferred to Mendota Mental Health Center in Madison where he died years later of lung cancer. Gein's story became the basis of the book *Psycho* by Robert Bloch, which was made into the movie of the same name by Alfred Hitchcock. Gein was the inspiration for several other horror movies, including *The Texas Chainsaw Massacre* and *Silence of the Lambs*, among others. His house was destroyed in a suspicious fire in 1958 and his gravesite is now unmarked.

PLATTEVILLE: Home of the World's Largest Man-Made M

Driving anywhere near Platteville around the University of Wisconsin-Platteville's Homecoming time, travelers may be astounded to see a large burning M on the distant horizon. Visible from three states (Wisconsin, Iowa, and Illinois) the world's largest man-made M is just outside of the city on Platteville Mound. It is made of four tons of whitewashed rock. The letter is 241 feet high and 214 feet across and is maintained by students at the university, which was the Wisconsin Mining School in its early days. The M is for mining, not for Platteville, lest there be any confusion. Kerosene lanterns are lit on the M at Homecoming every year and in the spring for the annual M-Ball. It was originally constructed in 1937. The owner of the land donated the entire mound to the university in 1960. Next to the M, there are 280 steps leading to the top of the mound where one can get a great view of the surrounding countryside.

PLYMOUTH: Cheese Capital of the World

Cheese Capital of the World is quite the bold claim to make for any city in America's Dairyland. Plymouth claimed the title all the way back in the early part of the 20th century. There were so many cheese producers in the southern part of the town that locals referred to the area as Cheeseville. There were manufacturers in other parts of the city, too. In 1918 the Wisconsin Cheese Exchange was formed in Plymouth, which later became the National Cheese Exchange. It worked much like the Stock Exchange, but with trading of cheese instead of stocks, and effectively helped determine the price of cheese throughout the country. The exchange moved to Green Bay in 1975 and cheese trading was later moved to the Chicago Mercantile Exchange. By the 1930s there were dozens of cheese factories and related industries in Plymouth. It was enough to proclaim the city the Cheese Capital of the World by 1940. While most of the Cheeseville producers have since gone out of business there are still several large cheese companies that make the city their home. At the site of the former Wisconsin Cheese Exchange there is a 20-foot-tall fiberglass cow named Antoinette that was erected to honor the city's dairy heritage. Plymouth's newest event is the Cheese Capital Festival, with a cheese-themed parade and plenty of cheese-related activities. Sponsored by Sartori Cheese, the city also has a New Year's Eve Cheese Drop to bring in the new year. It's similar to the Times Square ball drop, but cheesier.

PONIATOWSKI: Exact Center of the Northern Half of the
Western Hemisphere

This is another of the geographical claims to fame in the state. Located in Marathon County, Poniatowski is halfway between the North Pole and the equator, as well as halfway between the Greenwich Median and the International Dateline. The exact spot is a few miles out of town on Meridian Road. Once at the site, which is a Marathon County park, a path leads to the marker laid in the ground denoting the point that is 45 degrees north and 90 degrees west. There are several signs at the site, which give more information for those interested. One provides details on the other three 45x90 locations around the world. Two of them are located in the oceans and the last is in a mountainous, difficult to reach area of China, so the one in Poniatowski is the only easily accessible one. Another sign explains latitude and longitude. Yet another tells about John Gesicki, the Poniatowski resident who promoted the importance of the site. Some scholars have suggested that the actual spot should be about ten miles further north due to the earth not being perfectly round. While the spot is 45x90, they say it is not the exact center of the northwest hemisphere. Those who reach the marker can stop by the nearby Wausau/Central Wisconsin Visitor Center, sign the logbook, and get a free commemorative medallion that proclaims them a member of the 45x90 club.

POPLAR: Hometown of Richard Bong

Richard Bong was a major in the United States Army Air Force (now the United States Air Force) during World War II and is to this day America's all-time leading war ace. He shot down two enemy aircraft in his very first battle in the war and by the end of it had taken down 40 enemy aircraft, more than any other American pilot in history. He won the Congressional Medal of Honor, Distinguished Service Cross, Distinguished Flying Cross, Silver Star, an Air Medal, and many other honors for his efforts. He was known as the Ace of Aces. Bong grew up in Poplar, showing an early interest in airplanes and model plane building in his youth. Ironically, the war ace died in a crash while conducting a test flight of a jet plane. It happened on the same day in 1945 that the U. S. dropped the atomic bomb on

Hiroshima. He was buried in his hometown of Poplar. The United States gifted a P-38 airplane to the town which served as a memorial for many years. It fell into disrepair and was eventually moved to the Richard I. Bong Veterans Historical Center in Superior. Bong was posthumously inducted into the National Aviation Hall of Fame in 1986 and the Wisconsin Aviation Hall of Fame in 1987. There are many things named after him, including the airport in Superior, Bong Recreation Area in southern Wisconsin, and at least a couple bridges, one in Superior and one in Annandale, Australia.

PORTAGE: Birthplace of Frederick Jackson Turner
Hometown of Zona Gale
Boyhood Home of John Muir
Birthplace of Margery Latimer

Most small towns do not have even one currently famous or historically important person born or raised there, but Portage can claim several. Though less known today, all were significant in their time.

Frederick Jackson Turner was a well-respected historian whose most famous work, the 1893 essay, 'The Significance of the Frontier in American History," influenced the study of American history for generations. He won the Pulitzer Prize in 1933 for his collection of essays, *The Significance of Sections in American History*. His frontier thesis posited that what is known as the American character was due not to the settled population of the eastern states, but due to the continuous westward frontier expansion, where old ways gave way to new. Because of moving further into the wilderness, frontiersman had to develop new ways of dealing with the wild land and became a new kind of American. Turner's influence lasted for decades. His theories have fallen out of favor over the last several decades because he focused on white men taming the frontier while ignoring class, women, people of color, and others who also advanced westward, as well as the people who lived there before white settlers started their westward expansion. Still, he probably had a greater impact on the study of American history, and particularly westward expansion, than most any other noted historian.

The first woman to win the Pulitzer Prize for Drama was Zona Gale of Portage for her stage adaptation of her own novel, *Miss Lulu*

Bett, in 1921. Gale had previous success as a short story writer and novelist who used her hometown of Portage where she lived and wrote as a resource for her fiction. Her first short story sale occurred when she was only 16. While she went away to college and lived in New York City for a time, she moved back to Portage in 1904 when she was 30. Her early writing realistically and successfully captured life in small-town America. Much of her later work was based upon her growing mystical beliefs and was not received favorably by critics or the public. In her later life she turned more toward political activism, working for women's equality, peace, and ending racial prejudice. Gale's home in Portage was gifted to the city upon her death, appropriately served as a library for years, and is now home to the Museum at the Portage. Both Turner and Gale have state historical markers in the city.

Born in Scotland, John Muir's family moved to a farm outside of Portage when he was 11 years old. He wrote of his childhood in the book, *The Story of My Boyhood and Youth*, which described his awakening love of the environment. Muir became known as the father of the national park system and one of the greatest environmentalists of all time. He is credited with being responsible for the creation of Yosemite, Grand Canyon, Sequoia, and several other beloved national parks. In 1892 he was one of the founders and the first president of the Sierra Club, which to this day is one of the leading climate change and environmental organizations in the world. Muir has been inducted into the Wisconsin Conservation Hall of Fame. The Muir family farm is a National Historic Landmark.

Portage (and maybe the rest of the world) seems to have forgotten another writer who was born there. Feminist and writer Margery Latimer was the author of two novels and two short story collections in the late 1920s and early 1930s. The books were highly regarded at the time. She died in childbirth at only 33 years old, cutting short her promising career. Although their writing was very different, Zona Gale was a mentor for the younger Latimer.

PORT WASHINGTON: Home of the World's Largest One Day Outdoor Fish Fry

Wisconsin is known for its Friday night fish fries. Port Washington decided to take that a step further and create the largest one of all, albeit on a Saturday. Dubbed Fish Day, the event is a festival of music and entertainment, though the central theme has always been fish, appropriate for the state that probably has more fish fries and fish boils than anywhere else on earth. The event started in 1964, but news reports in 2023 had organizers saying it was being put on hiatus, due mostly to lack of funding and volunteers, with no indication of when or if it might be back. The event has drawn thousands of attendees in the past and proceeds have gone back into the community through various service organizations. In 2022, though the event had been expanded to two days, many of the highlights had been reduced or eliminated, such as the fireworks, helicopter rides, and the carnival.

POTOSI: Catfish Capital of Wisconsin
             Home of the World's Largest Cone-Top Beer Can

Noted in the *Guinness Book of World Records* as having the World's Longest Main Street without an Intersection, Potosi instead lays claim as the Catfish Capital of Wisconsin. The town rests alongside the Mississippi River. Fishing is a big activity in the region and besides other species, the area is known for its catfish. While some eschew the catfish as a bottom feeder, those along the granddaddy of rivers know how good it can taste and know many ways of serving it up. Of course, the catfish title comes with a Catfish Festival. Highlights include the bean bag and euchre tournaments, the kids' mini tractor pull, the crowning of the Little Miss Catfish Queen, and the annual firemen's catfish dinner.

The world's largest cone-top beer can stands near the Potosi Brewery, which in the 20th century was the fifth largest brewery in Wisconsin. After 120 years, the brewery ceased production in 1972 and sat idle for about three decades with the buildings falling into disrepair. It was purchased in 1997 and renovation began. In 2008 it reopened as the National Brewery Museum and it now attracts tens of thousands of visitors from all over the world every year. The site is brewing beer once again at a microbrewery associated with the museum. Next to the brewery, the oversized beer can has the old Potosi Beer label on it and is modeled after the classic Potosi cone-top beer cans from the heyday of the brewery. It's over 40 feet tall and on the back of the can is an inscription that notes, "2,319,242 fl.

Oz." It opens on the bottom to function as a bar during special events. The beer can was originally a silo on what used to be the Potosi Brewery farm.

PRAIRIE DU CHIEN: Wisconsin's Second Oldest City

Green Bay was established as a trading post in 1634, which makes it the oldest European settlement in Wisconsin, but Prairie du Chien is a somewhat close second. Explorers Jacques Marquette and Louis Jolliet came to the site of the present-day city in 1673 and it soon became the center of the fur trade. Today there is a fur trade museum, as well as many other historical sites, especially on St. Feriole Island, which is where Prairie du Chien started. The island was the site of the only battle to take place in Wisconsin during the War of 1812. An encampment and reenactment are held every summer. It was also the site of Fort Crawford, where Black Hawk surrendered to end the Black Hawk War and several other treaties were signed. Elsewhere on the island is the site of Villa Louis, a beautiful Victorian mansion that became Wisconsin's first State Historic Site in 1952. Not too far from Villa Louis is the Trail of Presidents, which is a short walk with markers noting 22 American Presidents who visited the city, as well as two others—Confederate President Jefferson Davis and Mexican President Vicente Fox. Fox attended the local Catholic school, Campion, as a youth. The newest addition on the island is a sculpture park honoring area historical figures. The goal is to have nearly 30 sculptures when the park is completed. Currently there are six: Dr. William Beaumont and son Israel, Black Hawk, Marianne La Buche, Victorian Lady, Emma Big Bear, and Julian Coryer. There is more history representing different eras in a small area on St. Feriole Island than almost any other place in the state.

PRAIRIE DU SAC: Cow Chip Capital of Wisconsin

Only in America's Dairyland could a city take such pride in hosting the state cow chip throw (or perhaps Beaver, Oklahoma, which lays claim as the *world's* cow chip throwing capital). Cow chips, or cow pies, for those who may not know, are dried piles of cow manure, and there are people who compete to see who can theow them the farthest every year at the Wisconsin State Cow Chip Throw. Surprisingly, cow chip throwing has a history going back as far as ancient Greece and events are held in many places, although it seems particularly appropriate in the state that leads the nation in cheese production and is second in milk production. Prairie du Sac has hosted the event since it was started in 1975 by the local Jaycees organization. Around 250 competitors and 40,000 attendees come to the two-day festival every year. Contestants can throw the chips however they desire. Many contestants throw them like a frisbee because of the similar shape, but old hands at the event suggest that throwing it more like a football or axe will yield better results. The current state record throw is 248 feet by Greg Neumaier, a record which has stood since 1991 (the Beaver, Oklahoma record throw, by the way, is 188.5 feet). Distances are measured by a team of land surveyors. One additional note: the State Legislature made the cow chip the "unofficial state muffin" in 1989.

PRESQUE ISLE: Walleye Capital of the World

Presque Isle is located in a county that features a seemingly endless number of lakes and dozens of rivers and smaller bodies of water. Presque Isle Lake's waters contain several species, including walleye, which are common in the lake. In the mid-20th century, a lumber company's abandoned mill pond was converted into a state fish hatchery and provided thousands of walleyes to lakes around the state. This led to the town being called the Walleye Capital of the World. The old mill pond located at present-day Pipke Park is now a lake and it still has a nice population of walleye for fishing. However, it is no longer used as a rearing pond for the species, and because of this, the walleye capital claim has fallen out of use. The town still hosts an annual walleye tournament in May, but has come up with a new slogan, Wisconsin's Last Wilderness..

PULASKI: Polka Capital of Wisconsin (or Polka Town, U. S. A.)

The official state dance of Wisconsin is the polka. It was signed into law by Governor Tommy Thompson in Pulaski in 1994. Czech, Polish, and German immigrants who settled in large numbers in the state brought the dance with them and it spread across the Badger state as it did in other parts of the country. Few Wisconsinites have not been exposed to the dance and to polka music at weddings or other events (in addition to the ever-present Chicken Dance). In Pulaski, a community founded by Polish immigrants and named after the Polish military leader Casimir Pulaski, polka is a huge part of the culture. There are a number of polka bands from the town which only has a population of just under 4,000 people. Even local monks from the Franciscan Monastery at Pulaski formed a band in the 1960s and shocked some members of the community by playing "In Heaven There Is No Beer" at their performances. The annual Pulaski Polka Days is a four-day celebration of the music and dance, drawing visitors from across the country and internationally. The music plays almost continuously for the entire four days, with around 20 different bands to enjoy. In addition to all the music and dancing, there is a Ms. Pulaski Polka Days contest, polka dance lessons, and as in other cities in Wisconsin, a Sunday morning polka Mass. The New Life Community Church also hosts a polka service. Polka Days are in July, but the city has polka music at Casimir Pulaski Days in March and throughout the year at bars, weddings, and in living rooms around the town.

$\mathcal{R}$

RACINE: The Most Danish City in America
                 Kringle Capital of the World

The most Danish City in America is not just an idle boast. A large number of Danes who came to America settled in Wisconsin and a majority of those ended up in Racine. By the mid-1800s, the Racine area had more Danish-born residents than any other area of the state. Some estimates put the number of Danes in Racine at about ten percent of the Danish immigrants in the entire country. Two manufacturers, J. I. Case and Mitchell Wagon, specifically recruited Danes to come to Racine and a large majority of their employees in the 19th century were of Danish heritage. Other companies also gladly took on the immigrants as employees. Danes who had come to Racine encouraged others to follow. Their influence permeates the city to this day..

One of the Danish influences in Racine is the kringle, an oval pastry made with several dozen layers of dough and a variety of fillings, usually topped off with icing. Fillings include fruit and nuts, but can include anything that the baker feels would provide a delicious treat. The word comes from an Old Norse word meaning oval, or circle. The kringles made in Racine today are a Danish-American version of the authentic Danish kringles that date back centuries. There are several bakeries in the city that make them fresh. In addition to the usual favorites, they typically create special varieties and flavors for holidays or at different times throughout the year. They ship throughout the world. The dessert is so well-known in Racine and throughout the state that the kringle was named the official state pastry of Wisconsin in 2013.

REDGRANITE: Home of Wisconsin's State Rock

Wisconsin has many official state symbols, including a state pastry and a state rock, red granite. It was first proposed by the Kenosha Gem and Mineral Society and was named the state rock in 1971 due to its abundance in Wisconsin, its value, and being native to the state. Red granite is mined in many different places around the state. The rock was found on farmland around the town first known as Sand Prairie in the 1800s. Because of the rock, the soil above it was thin and could not be used for farmland. Once quarry owners realized there were large deposits of red granite on several area farms, they bought the owners out and opened a quarry.in late 1889. Eventually Sand Prairie was renamed Redgranite because of the deposits, quarries, and importance to the local economy. The rock was typically used for paving, though some was sold for buildings, monuments, and other purposes. Today it is often used for kitchen countertops. Once road constructors started to use concrete or asphalt, the demand for the town's red granite fell off, as did the town's industry and population. The quarry in Redgranite has been used as a swimming hole since the 1960s.

REEDSBURG: Butter Capital of America

Wisconsin supports its dairy industry. Until 1967, it was illegal to sell colored margarine in the state and it is still illegal for restaurants to serve margarine instead of butter unless both are offered to patrons. It's likely the citizens of Reedsburg were okay with the ban on margarine. According to locals, in the latter half of the 20th century the local milk plant in Reedsburg produced more butter than any other place. It is why the city laid claim to being the Butter Capital of America. That's no longer the case, and the city seems to have relinquished the claim, but the people still celebrate those days with Butterfest, which has been held for more than 50 years. Started in 1971, the festival is held every June which, appropriately enough, is Dairy Month. The festival includes music, food, a carnival, tractor pull, demolition derby, parade, and the crowning of a king and queen. There is also a Run for the Butter race for children and adults.

RHINELANDER: Home of the Hodag
                 Birthplace of Dale Wasserman

The hodag is a mythical creature of Wisconsin's Northwoods, though those from Rhinelander might argue about the word mythical. It can be difficult to describe as different witnesses have reported varied descriptions of the beast. It has only been found around the Rhinelander area, so sightings have been few. Typically, a hodag is short and up to seven feet long, with horns on its head, a mouth full of large teeth and large fangs, sharp claws, and horns or spikes running down its back and the top of its tail. It was first reported in the late 1800s by area loggers. A local entrepreneur, Gene Shepard, toured with what he claimed was a live hodag, but ultimately had to admit that it was a hoax designed to fool the public and bring in money. Honoring its uniqueness to the area, the hodag is the nickname and mascot for the local high school. It is also the official symbol of the city of Rhinelander.

The hodag is not the only one native to the Rhinelander area. Playwright, screenwriter, and producer Dale Wasserman was born in Rhinelander in 1914, one of 14 children, and grew up to live the impossible dream. His parents were Russian immigrants and he was orphaned at nine years old. From Rhinelander, he was sent to an orphanage in South Dakota for some time, but ended up spending much of his adolescence on the road and riding the rails. He finally arrived in California, settled in Los Angeles, and started learning the theater business. A mostly self-taught man, he wrote around 80 plays and was best known for the stage adaptation of *One Flew Over the*

Cuckoo's Nest, the screenplay for *Cleopatra*, and the book for the hugely successful and popular musical, *Man of La Mancha*, for which he won the Tony award.

RICHLAND CENTER: Birthplace of Frank Lloyd Wright

While he was born in Richland Center, Frank Lloyd Wright's family did not stay in any one place too long when he was a child, moving to Iowa when he was two years old and continuing to move periodically throughout his early youth until ending up back in Wisconsin when he was 12 years old. Wright became one of the most renowned and influential architects of the 20th century. He was named the all-time greatest American architect by the American Institute of Architects—an organization he never joined—and his name is perhaps the most recognized name in architecture. Among his better-known works are Fallingwater, a residence built around a 30-foot-tall waterfall in Pennsylvania; the Robie house in Chicago; the S. C. Johnson headquarters in Racine; Taliesin, his own home in Spring Green; the Imperial Hotel in Tokyo; and the Guggenheim Museum in New York City. An early Wright building designed in 1915 and built over the following years can still be seen in Richland Center. Wright was well-known around southern Wisconsin for his failure to pay debts. The A. D. German Warehouse was designed by Wright in exchange for the forgiveness of an unpaid debt to Mr. German. While it is not one of his most famous works, it is the only Wright-designed building in Richland Center, the only warehouse designed by him, and is one of his many buildings listed on the National Register of Historic Places.

RIPON: Birthplace of the Republican Party
          Birthplace of Carrie Chapman Catt
          CookieTown U. S. A.

Originally founded as a Utopian socialist community, Ripon ironically lays claim as the birthplace of the Republican Party. While a couple other towns in other states make the same claim, Ripon is generally recognized as the more likely candidate. In 1854 a group of men met in the city's first public school, known as the Little White Schoolhouse, in response to the admission of Kansas and Nebraska as slave states. While the men were of varying political parties going into the meeting, they decided they all had to oppose slavery in a unified manner and called themselves Republicans after the meeting. Horace Greeley, the famous editor of the *New York Tribune*, was a friend of one of the men at the meeting, Alan E. Bovay, and popularized the term "Republican" elsewhere in the country. It is believed that Ripon later became a stop on the Underground Railroad. The schoolhouse is on the National Register of Historic Places and is now a museum. In 2023 a plan was developed to move the schoolhouse to a new location, which could cause it to be delisted from the National Register.

Another kind of political activism sparked Carrie Chapman Catt, internationally known women's suffragette, who was born and lived seven years in Ripon. She was one of the founders and first president of the League of Women Voters. She headed the National American Woman Suffrage Association two times, from 1900-1904 and again from 1915-1920. She was the first president of the International Woman Suffrage Alliance from 1904-1923. Catt played a huge role in earning women the right to vote through her work from 1900 to 1920. The 19th amendment to the Constitution, guaranteeing women the right to vote, was passed in 1920. After that right was secured Catt became active in the cause of international peace. A state historical marker on Catt is located at Pedrick Wayside on the corner of Union Street and West Fond du Lac Street.

Finally, Ripon became CookieTown U. S. A. in the early 1990s, when Governor Tommy Thompson made it official by proclamation. He did so after workers at a local cookie plant created the world's largest chocolate chip cookie, a record that made the *Guinness Book of World Records*. The cookie was 34 feet in diameter and filled with almost four million chocolate chips. Ripon was the home of Rippin' Good Cookies, which for many years was the city's largest employer. A little more than 20 years after the Governor's proclamation both of Ripon's two cookie plants were shuttered by new owners and about 350 people lost their livelihoods while Ripon lost a part of its heritage. Cookies had been made in the town for more than 80 years before the plant closings. Along with the closure of the plants, a popular outlet store closed and a local celebration, Cookie Daze, was eventually discontinued.

RUDOLPH: Home of the Rudolph Grotto Gardens and Wonder Cave

Wisconsin has a number of religious shrines, folk sculpture collections, and grottos. One of the better-known ones is the Rudolph Grotto Gardens and Wonder Cave. The gardens sit on five acres of land next to St. Phillip's Catholic Church. One can wander a path past depictions of each of the 14 Stations of the Cross, representing parts of Jesus' journey to his death on Calvary. There are also the Seven Sorrows of Mary, St. Jude's Chapel, a museum, and gift shop. The Wonder Cave is designed to represent the catacombs and has 26 shrines within its walls. The entire site was the realization of a promise of Father Philip Wagner who was the pastor of the local church. As a young man he had prayed for recovery from ill health while visiting Lourdes in France. He had promised that if his health recovered he would build a shrine in honor of Mary. The first shrine, completed in 1927, was the Lourdes Shrine. More shrines and other additions to the site were added over several decades. Some of the more unusual elements at the gardens are the world's smallest stone church, a cabin celebrating Wisconsin in miniature, lighthouses, a war memorial, and a sundial. The site also includes a picnic area.

S

ST. GERMAIN: Home of the Snowmobile Hall of Fame

The snowmobile is so important in northern Wisconsin that there are two halls of fame, the International Snowmobile Hall of Fame in nearby Eagle River and the Snowmobile Hall of Fame in St. Germain. Appropriately situated on Sled World Boulevard the Snowmobile Hall of Fame celebrates the history of snowmobiles and their riders. The St. Germain hall is a museum that features displays on both the recreational and competitive racing aspects of the ice sleds. The museum owns well over 100 snowmobiles, including historic models and championship sleds. It also houses snowmobile gear, associated products, toys, and many other items including photographs and historic artifacts. The museum includes a library. The Hall of Fame honors significant figures in racing, manufacturing, and other aspects of the vehicle and its use. Inductions have been held every February since 1988 and there have been over 50 inductees over the years.

SAUK PRAIRIE: Where Eagles Soar
                       Birthplace of August Derleth
                       Wisconsin's Oldest Incorporated Village

Where Eagles Soar sounds like a generic boast or a consumer-tested marketing slogan, but Sauk City and its sister city, Prairie du Sac (together generally known as Sauk Prairie) have more eagles soaring than most places around the state of Wisconsin. Because of the hydroelectric dam in Prairie du Sac, bald eagles have come to the area for many years as the water below the dam stays open in the winter and allows eagles to capture fish during the cold season. Up to 200 or more eagles settle in the area from the start of winter to the start of spring. There are many viewing areas set up for people to spot the eagles. Officials ask that visitors stay in their cars to view the eagles as they are easily frightened when humans approach on foot. Every January the twin cities host Eagle Watching Days featuring eagle watching, tours, educational presentations, and birds of prey shows.

August Derleth is probably best remembered for publishing the books of H. P. Lovecraft through his publishing house, Arkham Press. The publishing house was co-founded with his friend and fellow writer, Donald Wandrei. Without Arkham Press, Lovecraft may have never had an influence on horror and fantasy fiction, and may not even be remembered at all. Arkham House also published Ray Bradbury's first book. Derleth himself was a well-known writer in his day and is often considered Wisconsin's most prolific, and some say best, writer. He had more than 150 books to his credit and in many genres. He wrote horror, history, young adult, poetry, fiction, essays, journals, and much of it, if not most, was based on his hometown of Sac Prairie, his favored term for the twin cities of Sauk City and Prairie du Sac where he grew up. His best-known and best work is generally considered to be *Walden West*, a paean to the land and people he loved and knew so well. It was part of a large series of books about the area called the Sac Prairie Saga. Derleth was born in Sauk City and returned to his home after college, choosing it as his place of residence and the place where he wrote so much of his work.

His childhood home and the house he built with his success as a
writer, which he named "Place of Hawks," both still stand but are not
open to the public. The August Derleth Society was founded in Sauk
City in 1978 with the aim of studying and promoting Derleth's
writing. It is housed in the August Derleth Center on Water Street in
Sauk City. The city has developed a walking tour around Derleth. It
has also hosted a Walden West Festival featuring speakers and
displays about Derleth and his career. The state has erected a
historical marker about him, located outside the August Derleth
Society headquarters on the corner of Water and Hemlock Streets in
Sauk City.

Sauk City had already been around for more than a decade under
previous names, but incorporated as a village in 1854, making it the
oldest incorporated village in the state. The fact is marked on the
city's official logo.

SAYNER: Birthplace of the Snowmobile

Carl Eliason, a 25-year-old tinkerer, invented the first
snowmobile in Sayner in 1924. He called it a motor toboggan and
received a patent for it three years later. It was essentially a toboggan
fitted with a small boat motor and skis, which were turned with ropes
from the sled. After getting his patent, he built and sold more than
three dozen of the machines before selling the manufacturing rights.
Though it was a distant relative to the modern snowmobile it is
considered the first snowmobile, as its basic features are still part of
today's snowmobiles. The city proudly proclaims itself the Birthplace
of the Snowmobile, a machine that is to some in Wisconsin and the
upper Midwest as important as the car. A century later, the Vilas
Historical Museum houses Eliason's original motor toboggan among
its other local history items, as well as a number of outboard motors,
invented in Wisconsin by Ole Evinrude. The local snowmobile club,
the Sayner-Star Lake Barnstormers, created the county's first
snowmobile trail system and maintains it every year. Vilas County has
over 600 miles of snowmobile trails for winter enthusiasts to enjoy.

SEYMOUR: Home of the Hamburger

Despite several claims, nobody really knows where the

hamburger originated, but Seymour is one of the many places that lay claim to being the birthplace of what could very well be America's favorite food item. According to local lore, 15-year-old Charlie Nagreen, later known as Hamburger Charlie, had made meatballs to sell at the first annual Seymour Fair way back in 1885, but sales were slow because people didn't want to take the time to stop and eat. Nagreen found some bread, smashed the meatballs between the bread, added onions, and sold them to go. It is said he called it the hamburger after Hamburg, Germany as there were many German settlers in the area. Locals say that he was the person who first called it the hamburger. The town has erected a statue of Hamburger Charlie and holds an annual Burger Fest to celebrate him, the hamburger, and its role in the town's history. Across the street from the Hamburger Charlie statue is a giant grill upon which a world record hamburger was made in 2001. That burger weighed over four tons and fed thousands of people. Nearby, the Seymour Community History Museum houses the world's largest collection of hamburger memorabilia. The collection belonged to Jeffrey Tennyson, author of the book, *Hamburger Heaven*. Upon his death, the collection was left to his friend, Monte Greges, who donated it to the city of Seymour so that others could enjoy it. The collection includes everything from hamburger salt and pepper shakers to burger-shaped radios to lunch pails and more, over 1,500 items in all.

SHEBOYGAN: Bratwurst Capital of the World
                       Freshwater Surf Capital of the World

While the hamburger may be America's favorite meat, Wisconsin's could very well be the bratwurst, or brat, as it is more commonly called. The brat is a sausage made of pork or beef, with added spices. It is bigger than a standard hot dog and tastes completely different. In Sheboygan it is what made the city famous as Sheboygan bratwursts are known all over the country. About half of the city's population can claim German heritage. Their ancestors brought sausage-making, and particularly bratwurst, with them when they came. There are several butchers and small markets that still make home-made brats and there are large manufacturing facilities in the area that make brats. The city started a Brat Fest back in the 1950s and in 1970 won a court case that allowed it to claim itself the

Bratwurst Capital of the World. The losing side in that case, Bucyrus, Ohio, now claims to be the Bratwurst Capital of America.

Brats are not the only world capital claim in Sheboygan, but the other one is a bit unexpected. When one thinks of surfing, usually Hawaii or California or even Australia might come to mind. Most people don't think of the Great Lakes, Wisconsin, or Sheboygan. But Sheboygan has gained a reputation as the Freshwater Surf Capital of the World. It is sometimes called the Malibu of the Midwest. Surfers come from all over the world to take advantage of Lake Michigan's waves when the wind kicks in a bit. The peak season for surfing Lake Michigan is fall and winter, so the cold water and conditions make it exhilarating surfing for adventure seekers. Wetsuits and other protective gear are essential when surfing the Great Lakes. Given the right conditions, surfers can put their boards in all year long, but the wind and waves tend to be much better as the colder weather settles into the area.

SHULLSBURG: Birthplace of the Badger Nickname
              Site of Wisconsin's Worst Mining Disaster
              Hometown of Callen Harty

Shullsburg is one of the oldest cities in the state, but being one of something is not enough of a claim to fame. Because the city is so old it does have another claim. The town was founded in 1827 when miners poured into the region for the lead rush. Southwestern Wisconsin had rich deposits of lead and zinc. The first miners who came to the area and to Shullsburg were known to dig into the hillsides for shelter and for the ore, earning them the nickname of badgers after the burrowing animal. There used to be a large billboard at the Highway 11 entrance to the town proclaiming the town in somewhat awkward wording to be the birthplace of Wisconsin's badger nickname. That sign was replaced at some point with a cleaner looking welcome sign with no claim. However, a historical marker located in the town's Badger Park put up by the Council for Wisconsin History notes, "This site is in the heart of the pioneer lead mining region, origin of Wisconsin's 'Badger' nickname. These hardy pioneers lived in caves dug into the sides of hills and thus came to be called 'badgers,' adopted in 1848 as our state nickname."

The worst mining disaster in Wisconsin history was at the Mulcahy Mine about a half-mile west of the city in 1943. Two men were repairing support beams when a cave-in occurred. Men from mines all around the area came to aid in the rescue effort and while they were trying to dig the men out another collapse happened. The two men in the initial cave-in were likely killed immediately. Six of the rescuers died in the second collapse and others were injured. The names of the eight miners who died are etched onto a memorial at Miners Memorial Park in downtown Shullsburg.

While he was born in Savanna, Illinois the author of the book, *Signs of Pride: Wisconsin Towns and Their Claims to Fame*, moved to Shullsburg when he was two years old and spent the rest of his childhood there. While the town does not have a sign about him, a museum, or any other recognition, he believes that once he finally finishes his "great American novel" the city will have no choice but to acknowledge his place in the town's history.

SIREN: Lilac Capital of Wisconsin

Siren really has no more lilacs than any other place in Wisconsin, but there is another surprising reason for the lilac capital claim. The founder and first postmaster of Siren was a Swedish immigrant named Charles Segerstrom. He named the city Syren after lilacs he found near his new home. Syren is the Swedish word for lilac or lilac tree. The spelling of the name was changed to the present-day Siren by the United States Post Office, perhaps thinking the word was misspelled. The city has several businesses with the word lilac as part of the business name and at least one street, Lilac Lane. While there is no lilac festival, there is an annual St. Patrick's Day Parade and celebration, which includes a "Lucky Lilac" scavenger hunt.

SISTER BAY: Home of Al Johnson's Swedish Restaurant

While Al Johnson's Swedish Restaurant specializes in serving authentic Swedish recipes, the establishment is far more famous for goats grazing on the grass roof of the building which has attracted tourists for years. The goats (and the tourists) can be seen throughout the warm season in Wisconsin, which can be a few weeks in July or August, but generally runs from May to October. The Sister Bay

Advancement Association has an annual Roofing of the Goats Parade where the goats are led through the streets and eventually up to the restaurant's rooftop for the season. Stickers are purchased for a fundraiser for the local food pantry and placed along the route. If one of the goats poops on a sticker that person can win a prize. Once the goats are on the roof the annual Goat Fest is held at the restaurant. For those who can't be there Al Johnson's has installed a goat cam where viewers can watch the rooftop goats online.

SOLDIERS GROVE: Nation's First Solar Village

Over the course of much of its history the village of Soldiers Grove suffered periodic flooding as the Kickapoo River repeatedly overflowed its banks. At least nine floods damaged or devastated downtown Soldiers Grove in the first seven decades of the 20th century. In 1975 the federal government approved a levee, but the cost to the city was not economically feasible as Soldiers Grove would have been responsible for maintenance and didn't have the tax base needed to cover it. Finally, tired of floods and rebuilding, citizens of the community decided it would be better to rebuild on higher ground out of the floodplain and requested money that would have been spent for the levee to help with relocation efforts. The federal government approved the idea, but moved slowly on it. Three years later nothing had been done, and then the town was hit with a hundred-year flood, the worst one in its history, in 1978. That flood got the bureaucrats moving and the funds were finally released to start the relocation. Someone came up with another novel idea. If all of the downtown buildings were to be rebuilt, why not make all of the new buildings solar? That idea was accepted and when it was done, the rebuilt downtown made the town America's first solar village. And, by the way, two more historic hundred-year floods hit in 2007 and 2008, the 2007 flood topping the flood of 1978 as the worst in history, and the 2008 one topping 2007. The relocated solar village remained safe up the hill out of the floodplain.

SOMERSET: Inner Tubing Capital of the World

The Apple River is considered one of the best inner tubing rivers in the country. It is an extremely popular tubing river and has been for decades. The Somerset area along the Apple is where most people put their tubes in to enjoy the ride. While a Thai princess is sometimes considered the originator of inner tubing, nightclub owner David Breault of Somerset is credited with popularizing it in America in the 1940s. He and Somerset were featured in a *Life* magazine article about tubing and brought it to the attention of the country. A smart businessman, Breault provided the inner tubes at no charge, but it paid for itself with increased business at his establishment. A lot of tubers bought drinks and took them along to drink as they floated along the river and went back for more drinks after tubing. These days there are several outfitters where rentals are available. The tubing ride itself is varied as the first part of the ride is gentle and an easy float, and the last section has fast, wild rapids. The entire ride can take two and a half to three and a half hours. Some only do one half or the other.

SPARTA: Bicycling Capital of America
               Birthplace of Deke Slayton
               Home of the F.A.S.T. Corporation

A huge fiberglass high-wheeled bicycle, 32 feet tall, with a rider named Ben Bikin atop, is billed as the world's largest bike, and it's just one part of the reason Sparta calls itself the Bicycling Capital of America. The claim is mostly because Sparta is one end of the Elroy-Sparta Bike Trail, which was the country's first rails to trails bike trail. Rails to trails are bike trails that used to be railroad beds and were converted to bike trails. The Elroy-Sparta trail was opened to the public back in 1967. There are now almost 2,000 of these trails in the country, totaling over 20,000 miles, and there are hundreds more in progress. The Elroy-Sparta Trail connects to several other nearby bike trails. It is a bit over 32 miles long and features five towns, three 150-year-old tunnels, and diverse landscape from one end to the other. Because it was the first rail-to-trails bike trail in America, it has drawn visitors from all over the country, up to 60,000 a year. Due to flooding in 2018 the trail was closed for repairs and reopened again in 2022.

Deke Slayton was born in Sparta. Along with six other men, Slayton was selected to be one of NASA's first astronauts after his service as a pilot in World War II and the Korean conflict and several years as a test pilot. He was part of the Mercury 7 team put together in 1959. Slayton never made it into space as part of the Mercury team. Due to health concerns, he was grounded and did not make it into space until more than a dozen years later when his health had improved and he was named part of the crew on the Apollo-Soyuz mission, the first docking mission between the United States and Russia. While grounded, Slayton worked for NASA in many capacities, and he was the one who chose Neil Armstrong to be the first man to walk on the moon.

Combining the two claims to fame Sparta is home to the Deke Slayton Memorial Space and Bicycle Museum, which traces transportation from bicycles to space transport. The museum has a large number of bicycles, as well as memorabilia from Slayton's career. The highlight of the museum is a space rock from the moon, even though Slayton was never one of the astronauts to set foot on the moon.

While it is not promoted by either the city or the corporation, the grounds of the FAST Fiberglass company are a destination for many tourists. The initials stand for Fiberglass-Animals-Sculptures-Trademarks and the company is the leading manufacturer of fiberglass animals and figures used to advertise businesses or draw in curious customers, and has in recent years added water slides to its product line. It is the company that built the giant muskie in Hayward, Big Boys all over the country, large pink elephants, and most of the mice with cheese and other large fiberglass figures seen around the country. The lot behind the facility has drawn visitors from all over as it is a graveyard of discarded fiberglass figures. It is a funny, somewhat creepy, and altogether fascinating place to visit.

SPRING GREEN: Home of Taliesin
                     Home of The House on The Rock
                     Home of American Players Theatre

There are two vastly different and unusual architectural structures in the Spring Green area. The first is a Frank Lloyd Wright designed home which served as the architect's own home and studio. It is the third structure on the same site named Taliesin after the first two suffered fire damage. The building sits atop a ridge and the Welsh word Taliesin translates as Shining Brow. Taliesin is a National

Historic Landmark and in 2019 was named a UNESCO World Heritage Site, one of only a couple dozen in the United States. On the grounds are a number of buildings designed by Wright over several decades. He designed some of his most famous buildings while living there, including Fallingwater and the Guggenheim Museum. He founded a school for architects and taught apprentices at the site. Tours of varying lengths are offered.

While Taliesin is an internationally recognized work of architecture, the House on the Rock is an international tourist destination. The house, built by Alex Jordan, is not just a house. It is a complex of rooms featuring displays of Jordan's eclectic collections. Some displays feature antiques and valuable items and others appear to be nothing more than interesting bric-a-brac. In the center of the house is a large carousel which features over 250 animals and a couple thousand lights. In a far corner of the building is a display featuring a model of a giant whale. Another section features a recreation of a small town. The Infinity Room stretches out 218 feet over the valley below. At the far end is a window in the floor through which you can look down at the forest below. Around every corner of the House on the Rock is another surprise. The original house was built upon Deer Shelter Rock, a 200-foot-tall rock structure over the Wyoming Valley, and more rooms were added throughout the years. Today, the House on the Rock is one of the most popular tourist destinations in Wisconsin.

American Players Theatre is a company that specializes in the classics and is located in the woods outside of Spring Green. There is an amphitheater that seats over 1,000 audience members and a more intimate indoor theater. The company was founded by Charles Bright, Randall Duk Kim, and Anne Occhiogrosso in 1977 and produced its first play in 1980. Five years later the company was nominated for a Tony award for Outstanding Regional Theater and in 2011 was named Theater Company of the Year by the *Wall Street Journal* theater critic Terry Teachout. He also called it the best classical theater company in the United States.

SPRING VALLEY: Home of the Largest Earthen Dam in the Midwest

Like Soldiers Grove and many other Wisconsin cities situated along rivers Spring Valley's early history features many floods, including several major ones, over the course of decades. Some years saw multiple floods. The town suffered a historic flood in 1942 with up to 20 feet of water in parts of the town. It almost wiped the town out of existence. Somehow, nobody was seriously injured and no lives were lost. Worse than all the others, it was another of the constant battles with the Eau Galle River and nearby creeks overflowing their banks. Eventually it was decided to do something about it. Built as part of a flood control project, the Eau Galle Dam is a short distance north of Spring Valley and is the largest earthen dam in the Midwest. It was completed by the Army Corps of Engineers in 1968, part of a project begun in the late 50s, to stem the repeated flooding and to prevent another catastrophic flood like the one in 1942. Since then, the residents have been spared from the occasionally raging river. The dam created a reservoir named Lake George, which is now a popular recreation area for the citizens and nearby residents. Spring Valley hosts Dam Days annually during the third weekend of September to celebrate the dam and how it saved the city. There may be no other town that celebrates its dam in such a dam fine way, but there may be no other town so dependent on their dam either.

STEVENS POINT: Home of the Wisconsin Conservation Hall of Fame

Wisconsin has produced some of the leading environmentalists in American history. The Wisconsin Conservation Hall of Fame in Stevens Point honors environmental pioneers from conservation's early days to modern contributors working to save the environment. Among the more well-known honorees in the hall are Owen Gromme, wildlife painter; Increase Lapham, naturalist; John Muir, father of the national parks system and founder of the Sierra Club; Gaylord Nelson, former governor and senator and founder of Earth Day and Earth Week; and Sigurd Olson, author and activist. These are just some of the more than 100 inductees in the hall. The hall is located in the Visitor Center at the Schmeeckle Reserve, a nature conservancy on the campus of UW-Stevens Point.

STOCKBRIDGE: Sturgeon Capital of the World

Wisconsin has an incredibly large selection of fish capitals. Stockbridge lays claim to be the Sturgeon Capital (sometimes Center), not just of Wisconsin, but of the World. The town is located on Lake Winnebago, the largest inland lake in a state with 15,000 lakes. The lake has one of the largest and healthiest populations of lake sturgeon in North America. These fish can grow up to around 200 pounds and live to 100 years old. They were around when dinosaurs roamed the earth and have hardly changed since that time. In the 19th and 20th centuries, sturgeon were overfished, spawning routes blocked by dams, and many lost due to pollution. Populations were decimated elsewhere and were in danger in the state, but there has historically been strong state management of lake sturgeon in Wisconsin, which is why the population of the fish is still doing well in Lake Winnebago. As early as 1915 the state banned all sturgeon harvesting to protect them. The lake is one of only two places in America where spear fishing of sturgeon is allowed, albeit for a short season in February. Spear fishing of sturgeon was originated by the Native Americans who lived in Wisconsin first. After the annual spearing season, Stockbridge, which was named after an area tribe, hosts a sturgeon banquet where participants can share their fishing stories (listeners get to decide whether to believe them or not, but will likely enjoy the tales one way or the other), eat a nice dinner, and support and applaud the award winners.

STOUGHTON: Birthplace of the Coffee Break

Stoughton claims to have invented the coffee break as far back as 1880, appropriately enough on Coffee Street. The town was about 80 percent Norwegian and Coffee Street itself was nearly 100 percent at the time. It is said that Norwegian women who were hired to work at one of the tobacco warehouses did so in exchange for an agreement for a few minutes each morning and afternoon to take a quick break. This allowed them to run home and check on their children and any food that might be cooking, and to grab a quick cup of coffee to help keep them going through the day. Competitors to the claim include a tiemaker in Denver, but their story takes place during World War II, and a metal products manufacturer in Buffalo,

New York, but their claim is also well after Stoughton's, in the early 1900s. Stoughton celebrates its claim every August with the Coffee Break Festival. Corporate sponsorships of the festival start at the Cappuccino Level, then move upward to Latte Level, Mocha Level, and Mug Level. Among the usual festival events there is also a coffee brew-off and a bean spitting contest. Plenty of coffee is available for anyone who may need a quick pick-me-up.

STURGEON BAY: Shipbuilding Capital of the Great Lakes

Most people don't think of the upper Midwest as a shipbuilding stronghold, but it is a time-honored tradition in Wisconsin which is bordered on three sides by water—the Mississippi River to the west, Lake Superior to the north, and Lake Michigan to the east. Once a ship is built it can travel the St. Lawrence Seaway and through multiple locks to get from the Great Lakes to the Atlantic Ocean. Sturgeon Bay is located on the Door County Peninsula, which juts out into Lake Michigan. Ships have been built there since 1918. In the 1970s and 1980s many huge lake freighters were built there. Now called Bay Shipbuilding, ships are still built in Sturgeon Bay. The parent company, Fincantieri Marine Group, opened up two new buildings in 2021 which are climate-controlled and will allow them to continue building ships well into the future. It is the largest shipyard on the Great Lakes. The focus now is on building barges, tugs, tankers, and offshore support vessels. It also serves as a repair facility for Great Lakes freighters. One day a year the Sturgeon Bay Rotary Club offers tours of Bay Shipbuilding. In some years, the tours include other related sites, such as the Door County Maritime Museum. The museum details the maritime history of the county and also offers tours of a restored tugboat, the John Purves, and a lighthouse tower.

SUMPTER: Home of Dr. Evermor's Sculpture Park

Dr. Evermor, whose real name was Tom Every, built an entire sculpture garden out of found metal and other materials in the Town of Sumpter.. It is a fascinating site with a giant time machine called the Forevertron as the focal point. The Forevertron is claimed to be the largest scrap metal sculpture in the world at 50 feet high and 120 feet long, and it's pretty amazing to see. Along the paths of the park visitors encounter a giant bird orchestra with incredibly tall metallic birds playing a variety of musical instruments. There are dozens of the birds and many of them nearing 20 feet tall. On the ground closer to one's feet are a variety of large insects and other creatures crawling about the park. The Forevertron has been featured on television programs and the park is considered by many to be one of the must-see sculpture environments in Wisconsin.

SUN PRAIRIE: Groundhog Capital of the World
                    Hometown of Georgia O'Keefe

While most people think of Punxsutawney Phil as the most famous of the many groundhogs around North America that predict the weather, Sun Prairie calls itself the Groundhog Capital of the World and boasts of their prognosticator, Jimmy the Groundhog. While Phil has been appearing every Groundhog Day since the late 1800s, Sun Prairie's tradition on Groundhog Day has only been around since 1948, Wisconsin's centennial year. Apparently, however, it never occurred to Punxsutawney officials to claim to be the Groundhog Capital of the World, so when their local paper dismissed Sun Prairie and its groundhog, Sun Prairie countered by laying claim to the title, which was entered into the Congressional record. In addition, Sun Prairie claims that Jimmy's forecasting has been much more accurate than Phil's over the years, 89 percent for Jimmy and less than 50 percent for Phil, though Punxsutawney may dispute those figures. In 2015 Jimmy made national headlines and maybe supplanted Phil a bit on the news cycles when he bit the mayor on the ear during the annual Groundhog Day celebration.

Sun Prairie is the birthplace and hometown of Georgia O'Keefe, one of the most successful and important American artists of the 20th century. She was born on a farm near Sun Prairie in 1887 and most of her childhood was spent growing up there, with about a one-year stint in Madison, and a move out of state when she was 15. She received art lessons as a child and her interest in art was encouraged. Once she graduated from high school, she was determined to make her name as an artist. She studied at the Art Institute of Chicago and secured her first exhibit in New York in 1916. For a while she became a college art teacher and then resumed working full-time as an artist, changing her style and becoming famous for her vibrant, colorful depictions of flowers, cacti, animal skulls, and other images from the desert southwest. She permanently moved to New Mexico in 1949, but had been visiting and spending her summers there for 20 years before that. Today in Sun Prairie there is a street named after her, a state historical marker, and a Georgia O'Keefe room in the Sun Prairie Historical Library and Museum.

SUPERIOR: Home of A World of Accordions Museum

In a state that named the polka as its state dance, a museum dedicated to accordions makes a lot of sense, at least accordion to some. At A World of Accordions Museum in Superior, visitors can see the 1,300 accordions owned by the institution, including one-of-a-kind instruments. The library houses recordings and books. As part of its mission, the museum has a training program to certify students in accordion repair. The museum also has a concert hall that seats 1,000 and is used for a concert series featuring some of the world's best accordion players. Frankie Yankovic would be proud. Note: Frankie is no relation to Weird Al Yankovic, though Weird Al may be proud, too.

T

TAYCHEEDAH: Sheepshead Fishing Center of the World

Sheepshead is one of the most popular card games in Wisconsin. It is also a species of fish, and not one of the most popular. Sheepshead are strange-looking fish with human-like teeth. They have vertical stripes and are generally up to about 17 inches long, though they can grow longer. They are common in the Americas and Taycheedah, located on the southern edge of Lake Winnebago, has made a claim as the Sheepshead Fishing Center of the World, though it is not certain why, there are plenty of sheepshead in the lake. Perhaps all of the other major Wisconsin species had already been claimed and made capitals by other cities. Most anglers do not set out to catch sheepshead. They tend to get caught while fishing for other more popular varieties like walleye, bass, bluegill, and others, and most often get tossed back into the water. While they are edible most people do not.

TIMM'S HILL: The Highest Point in Wisconsin

Like Long Lake, this is one of the listings that is not a town, but still deserves some recognition. Timm's Hill, located in a Price County park with the same name, is the highest point in Wisconsin. The closest town is Ogema. Instead of claiming Timm's Hill, Ogema's slogan is "Our town can be your town, too." That might attract a few new residents, but probably not a lot of tourists. While Timm's Hill pales in comparison to so many states that have mountains, for Wisconsin 1,951 feet above sea level is getting up there. The state is just outside the bottom ten for highest elevation in the country. For those not afraid of heights there is an observation tower that affords a scenic view of the surrounding forests, as well as Bass Lake down the hill.

TOMAH: Hometown of Frank King

Frank King was the award-winning cartoonist who created the famed "Gasoline Alley" comic strip, a staple of American newspapers throughout much of the 20th century. Premiering in 1918 the strip is still running with new artists producing it and is the longest running American comic strip ("The Katzenjammer Kids" ran longer, but is no longer in production). "Gasoline Alley" won many awards over the years and also made history as the first comic strip in which the characters aged along with the readers. No others had naturally aging characters before "Gasoline Alley." While Cashton was his birthplace, Tomah claims King as its own. Superior Avenue is considered to be Gasoline Alley in the comic strip and many of the strip's characters were based on people King knew from Tomah. There are reminders all over the town that this is the place where Frank King was raised and graduated from high school. The Tomah Museum has information and displays on King, including his desk and some of his early artwork. He is buried alongside his wife at Oak Grove Cemetery in the town.

TWO RIVERS: Birthplace of the Ice Cream Sundae

There are several places around the country that claim to be the Birthplace of the Ice Cream Sundae, with Ithaca, New York, and Two Rivers as the two main contenders. Most food origins seem to have multiple competing towns that claim to be the ones to have originated the item and most are hard to prove. Ithaca has some pretty strong documentation for their claim. One strong reason to accept Two Rivers as the birthplace is that H. L. Mencken in the first supplement to his book, *The American Language,* had researched the word "sundae" and after reviewing several cities' claims to being the birthplace of the sundae determined that Two Rivers was the rightful claimant for the product and Manitowoc for the name. The story in Two Rivers is that the first ice cream sundae was a concoction created in the city in 1881 and originally sold only on Sundays. A customer, George Hallauer, asked Berner's Ice Cream Parlor owner Ed Berner to add chocolate to the top of his dish of ice cream. It went over well, and soon other customers asked for the same treat, which Berner decided to offer, but only as a Sunday special. After realizing the popularity of it, Berner eventually decided money could be made any day of the week, so he kept the name and dropped the restriction, also adding other flavors. From there, the popularity of the sundae spread. Billboards as you enter town note the claim, "Birthplace of the Ice Cream Sundae," while also including a subheading of "Get the Scoop in Town." Berner's shop has been recreated as part of the Washington House Museum, where visitors can order a number of different sundaes. The city celebrates its place in history every year with Sundae Thursday (yes, Thursday), with entertainment, an ice cream eating contest, and Sundaes for only a quarter.

WARRENS: Cranberry Capital of Wisconsin

Wisconsin is the nation's leading producer of cranberries and officially designated it as the state fruit in 2003. Warrens is located in the heart of the state's cranberry country, with several large cranberry companies located around the town. Cranberries grow in marshes which are flooded in the fall so that the berries float to the top and are then harvested. As the Cranberry Capital, Warrens developed the Wisconsin Cranberry Discovery Center, a museum and learning center. It is located in a former cranberry warehouse and is a warehouse of information on the cranberry and its importance to the Badger State. And being located in Wisconsin, it is also an ice cream shop, featuring cranberry ice cream. And being a museum, there is a gift shop featuring a dizzying array of cranberry products. Warrens is also host of the 50-year-old Warrens Cranberry Festival, which bills itself as the largest arts and crafts festival in the country and the largest cranberry celebration in the world. It is always held the last full weekend of September to celebrate the harvest and its importance to the region. It attracts up to 150,000 visitors every year, pumping a large amount of money into the local economy. Not bad for a town of less than 600 people. Like many small-town festivals, proceeds from the event are recycled into the community through various projects, scholarships, and local organizations. The festival has a parade, royalty, arts and crafts, and shopping galore. One of the highlights is tours of a cranberry marsh on both Friday and Saturday. Warrens is one of the towns along the Cranberry Highway, a self-guided 50-mile route through cranberry country. Visitors are encouraged to traverse it in the fall when the bright red cranberry marshes pose themselves against the green, yellow, orange, and brown leaves of autumn.

WASHINGTON ISLAND: One of the Oldest and Largest Icelandic Communities in the United States

Washington Island is the largest island of Door County and is located just northeast of the Door County peninsula. Much of Door County has Scandinavian roots, especially Norwegian and Danish. A great many early settlers to Washington Island were from the Scandinavian country of Iceland and many generations have lived on the island from that time to this day. Some say more Icelandic people settled on Washington Island than anywhere else outside of Iceland. The first great settlement of Icelanders in the United States was in Spanish Fork, Utah. The second was Washington Island. It started with four Icelandic men in their twenties who settled on the island in 1870, with others following. Descendants of the original four settlers can be found on the island today. Icelandic influence is evident on the island in the names of some streets and businesses, traditional Icelandic food, Icelandic (and other Scandinavian) flags, and even Icelandic horses.

WATERTOWN: Home of Carl Schurz
                      Home of the Nation's First Kindergarten

Carl Schurz was a liberal German who participated in the German Revolution of 1848 in which liberals tried to unify Germany as a democratic country and depose the aristocracy. They lost and people like Schurz went into exile, many of whom came to America and to Wisconsin. Schurz settled in Watertown in 1855, along with many other Germans. While most of the Watertown German settlers were Democrats, Shurz was an early Republican and anti-slavery man and convinced many to vote for Abe Lincoln for President by giving many speeches for the candidate. For his efforts he was rewarded with an appointment as minister to Spain. He left that position to join the Civil War effort and was appointed a general, fighting in some of the most famous battles of the war, including Gettysburg, the Second Bull Run, and Chancellorsville. After the war he left Wisconsin and continued his political life, serving a term in the United States Senate from Missouri and as Interior Secretary during Rutherford B. Hayes' administration. After leaving direct political involvement he became the editor of the *New York Evening Post* and *The Nation*. He was an early proponent of renewable forest resources and was named to the Wisconsin Conservation Hall of Fame because of those efforts.

Despite all of his accomplishments, Carl Schurz' wife's achievement is universally better known. In 1856 Margarethe Meyer Schurz founded the first kindergarten in America. She had worked with Fredrich Froebel, the man who first created the kindergarten in Hamburg, Germany, and she brought his ideas to America. Interestingly, her sister had founded the first kindergarten in England. The kindergarten building in Watertown still exists, but is no longer at its original location. The building was used for several purposes after the kindergarten closed, including a cigar factory, but was scheduled to be razed in 1956. Members of the local Watertown Historical Society worked to save it and restore it to its original condition. It was moved next to another historical building operated by the society, the Octagon House. It has been a museum since 1957 and is listed on the National Register of Historic Places.

WAUBEKA: Birthplace of Flag Day

The State of Wisconsin historical marker acknowledging the birthplace of Flag Day at Stony Hill School is located on the highway a half-mile out of Waubeka. Teacher Bernard Cigrand and his students held the first recognized Flag Day Ceremony on June 14, 1885, at the school. The teacher put a ten-inch flag in an inkwell and asked his students to write an essay on the meaning of the flag. Cigrand then campaigned for 31 years to have the American flag honored with its own special day. He selected June 14 as that was the date on which the Continental Congress adopted the stars and stripes design of our flag in 1777. He eventually won recognition of the holiday when Flag Day officially came into being on June 14, 1916. Waubeka was recognized as the birthplace of Flag Day by an act of Congress in 2004. Today the holiday is celebrated annually in Waubeka with a parade featuring over 100 units and a fireworks display at night. The National Flag Day Foundation is headquartered in Waubeka and works out of Stony Hill School, which has been restored and can be visited. Every one of the American flag iterations, as states were added, is on display. The Foundation sponsors an annual student essay contest, "What the American Flag Means to Me." Oddly, the sign proclaiming the city as the birthplace of Flag Day is a depiction of a Native American in full headdress wrapped in an American flag.

WAUKESHA: Birthplace of Les Paul

Born Lester Polfuss in Waukesha, Les Paul became one of the most important musical innovators of the 20th century. He developed the first solid body electric guitar, paving the way for the rock and roll era in music, although it is used in many genres. The Gibson Les Paul is one of the most famous of all guitars. The Gibson corporation honored Waukesha as one of its Guitar Towns, donating a number of ten-foot-tall guitars to decorate the city and help celebrate the importance of the guitar to the city. There are also a number of murals honoring the guitarist and inventor around downtown. Paul was already a well-known and respected guitarist and performer when the Gibson Les Paul was introduced in 1952. He had sold millions of records with his wife, Mary. They premiered their act at the 400 Club in Waukesha. Paul was also an early innovator in overdubbing, echo, tape delay, and multi-track recording. As a musician, he played jazz, blues, and country and has a permanent exhibit in the Rock and Roll Hall of Fame in Cleveland, Ohio. Paul's childhood home was located in the 300 block of West Saint Paul Avenue, but no longer exists. He is buried at Prairie Home Cemetery in Waukesha and his large monument there features a marker with a guitar and his signature.

WAUNAKEE: The *Only* Waunakee in the World

Waunakee is, in fact, the only Waunakee in the World.

WAUPUN: The City of Sculpture
                  Wild Goose Center of Wisconsin

While many Wisconsinites might think of Waupun as being the location of one of Wisconsin's most well-known prisons, others know of it for its art and its wildlife. According to the City of Waupun website, the city has one of the highest concentrations of public art per capita than almost anywhere else. It is all due to a local industrialist, Clarence Shaler, who donated several of his own sculptures to the city and also commissioned two others that he donated as well. Most famous of these is an iconic depiction of a Native American called "The End of the Trail," by sculptor James Earl Fraser. The sculpture represents the pain of Native Americans being pushed from their ancestral homes continually westward all the way to the Pacific Ocean. Fraser was the designer of America's buffalo nickel which was in use for 25 years in the early 20th century. The original "The End of the Trail" was sculpted in 1894 and the artist created several replicas. The sculpture in Waupun is the first bronze casting of it. Shaler's other commission was in memory of his wife, a memorial called "Recording Angel," by famed sculptor Larado Taft. It is located at Forest Mound Cemetery. Both statues are listed on the National Register of Historic Places. Seven other sculptures by

Shaler himself are placed throughout the city and a nearby cemetery.

Waupun is just a few miles from Horicon Marsh, a 33,000-acre wetland run in part by the state and in part by the federal government. Millions of birds migrate through every year, including anywhere from a quarter-million to a million Canada geese. The Wild Goose State Trail also runs along Horicon Marsh. Depictions of Canada geese have appeared on the letterhead and logos of the city of Waupun and of local businesses. Famous Wisconsin wildlife painter Owen Gromme painted Canada geese at Horicon Marsh. Surprisingly, no one has yet donated a goose sculpture to the city.

WAUSAU: Ginseng Capital of the World

Wausau is the seat of Marathon County, so it is in competition with its own county for the title of Ginseng Capital of the World. The city hosts the International Wisconsin Ginseng Festival, though some of the events are held in other parts of the county. While ginseng farms can be found around the county, there are a good number of them, including some of the largest, with Wausau addresses. Wausau also claims that while the Fromm Brothers of nearby Hamburg are credited with developing ginseng farming in central Wisconsin, it was really a man from Wausau, John Koehler, who was first. Koehler was born in Hamburg, but he spent most of his life as a businessperson in Wausau. He started farming ginseng in Wausau in 1901. Koehler wrote a book to help others get started called *The Ginseng Growers and Goldenseal Growers Handbook*. The book was published in Wausau in 1912. His ginseng farm was likely the earliest in the county, but the Fromm Brothers were more successful and eclipsed him in the history books and local legend.

WAUTOMA: Christmas Tree Capital of the World

There are several cities around the country that claim to be the Christmas Tree Capital and there are several states that produce more Christmas trees than Wisconsin, but it is big business in the Badger state, with more than 1.5 million trees sold annually. Wautoma has a number of Christmas Tree growers and in the early 1950s Kirk, one of the largest Christmas tree companies in the world, had a 10,000-acre tree farm there. The business has declined since then, but is still a significant part of the local economy. The Kirk Company also created a non-toxic, environmentally safe paint to color trees, which many of the producers use on their trees to sell them in various colors. It has proven popular with customers. The city, the Wautoma Rotary Club, and the local newspaper, the *Waushara Argus*, co-sponsor an annual Christmas parade which ends at a tree lighting ceremony.

WEBSTER: Sunfish Capital of Wisconsin

While Onalaska lays claim as the Sunfish Capital of the World, Webster sets its sights a little lower and claims to be the Sunfish Capital of Wisconsin. The town is about ten minutes from Sunfish Lake, which is primarily known for its panfish and largemouth bass according to the Wisconsin Department of Natural Resources. However, all of the area fishing spots have a wide variety of species to take, including sunfish. Both the Chamber of Commerce and the Village of Webster use an image of a sunfish on their web pages.

WEST ALLIS: Home of the State Fair
                Birthplace of Liberace

The Wisconsin State Fair used to move to different cities each year, starting with the first one in Janesville in 1851. West Allis was named the permanent home of the fair in 1892 and has hosted it ever since. The fair attracts about a million visitors a year and benefits the local economy. One of Wisconsin's favorite foods is the state fair cream puff. A Guinness record was set in 1991 when a 126-pound cream puff was created at the fair. The state fair also includes the WonderFair Wheel, the continent's largest traveling Ferris wheel.

West Allis is the birthplace of flamboyant pianist, singer, and all-around showman Liberace. The house where he was born still stands on South 60th Street in West Allis. Although born in West Allis, he grew up in West Milwaukee and went to West Milwaukee High School. Liberace started playing piano before he was even five years old. He played in a jazz band in high school, but started his career playing classical music. As he became better known he introduced pop music into his performances and would often combine classical pieces with lighter fare. As he took more control of his performances he started wearing flashy costumes with sequins and mink coats and his shows became more extravagant. Serious classical critics disparaged his music and shows as not being serious, but Liberace had decided to give his audiences, not the critics, what they wanted. Around that time he started billing himself as Mr. Showmanship. While it came out that he was gay after he died of complications from AIDS, he never publicly acknowledged his sexuality while he was alive and in fact won two lawsuits against publications that intimated he was gay. Liberace became one of the wealthiest performers of the 20th century, performing regularly in Las Vegas. He also toured extensively and often came back to the Milwaukee area to perform, often for benefits.

WEST SALEM: Birthplace of Hamlin Garland

Hamlin Garland was the 1922 Pulitzer-Prize winner for biography for his book, *Daughter of the Middle Border.* He was a well-respected regional writer who wrote more than 50 novels, among other works. His most famous books, the short story collection, *Main Travelled Roads*, and the *Middle Border* series, were written about the areas of Wisconsin and westward where he grew up. While he had moved away from his hometown, he returned in 1893 after his first writing success and bought a house where he lived and wrote until 1939, eventually moving out of state again. Garland's house has been preserved by the West Salem Historical Society and can be toured during the summer tourist season. It is on the National Register of Historic Places. A state historical marker about Garland is located at Swarthout Lakeside Park in West Salem. Another marker was put up at his gravesite in Neshonoc Cemetery in West Salem and was erected by the Hamlin Garland Junior Historical Club at West Salem Junior High School. The city celebrates Garland and its own history with Garland Days every year.

WILLOWS: Hometown of Barbara Roberts

Barbara Millicent Roberts was born in Willows, Wisconsin, and spent at least part of her childhood there. She had several careers and was known to be a doll. She was better known to the public by her nickname of Barbie rather than her given name of Barbara. Her long-time boyfriend, Ken, was also from Willows. Barbie was so well-known for her fashion sense and so popular with the general public that the toy company, Mattel, released a Willows, Wisconsin collection in 2015 that included Barbie in three outfits in memory of her hometown and simpler times. Included were a Cherry Pie Picnic costume, Homecoming Queen outfit, and a Soda Shop number. She eventually moved from Willows to Malibu, California, but never forgot her roots or her family that remained in her Wisconsin hometown.

WINNECONNE: The Town that Seceded from the State

Back in 1967, the town of Winneconne was left off of the official Wisconsin state map. The dot for the town was there, but the name was missing. It was first reported by the *Winneconne News*, which quipped "Map makers napping when they should have been mapping." Town officials were quick to react and demanded the state reissue the map with the town included, which the state declined to do. Supposedly Winneconne applied for admission to Canada, but they were ignored, so residents dumped Canadian whiskey into the Wolf River or possibly Lake Winneconne. Town officials decided to secede from Wisconsin and create their own nation. A flag was designed with the national symbols—a skunk, poison ivy, a dodo, and a sheepshead (the disturbing looking fish, not a sheep's head or the popular card game), all reflecting how they felt about the slight and how they felt their fellow Wisconsinites felt about them. In the center of the flag is a red star and the phrase, "We Like It—Where?" The secession was short-lived and the town rejoined the state a day later when the governor promised they would be put back on the map the next year. The flags can still be seen around town, especially when the whole thing is remembered every year in July during Winneconne's Sovereign State Days. The festival includes all the usual food and events of small-town festivals which you can find around the state, provided none of those towns are left off the official map or GPS.

WISCONSIN DELLS: Waterpark Capital of the World
                     Home of the Famous Wisconsin Ducks

The first waterpark in Wisconsin Dells was created in the 1970s. Now the Dells has more waterparks in one area than any other place in the world. Included are Mt. Olympus, which created North America's first rotating water slide, and Noah's Ark, which bills itself as the largest outdoor waterpark in America. The first indoor waterpark in the city was created in 1989 when a roof was put over the Polynesian Water Park Resort and that adaptation made it possible for the city to be a year-round destination. Being in Wisconsin it made sense to develop indoor waterparks so visitors could enjoy them even during the harsh winter months. These days, the Dells has a mix of indoor and outdoor waterparks with over 200 water slides, as well as pools, lazy river rides, and wave pools. The waterparks are also resorts that offer many other amenities for families to enjoy. Kalahari Resort created National Waterpark Day in 2017 and the resorts offer special activities to celebrate the day.

Originally used in World War II, the Wisconsin Ducks are amphibious vehicles that can travel on either land or water, which make them perfect vehicles for touring around a place like the Dells. They transport tourists through woods, into the Wisconsin River, past the incredible rock formations along the river and back to land again. While they never gain a great amount of speed they do make for an interesting excursion and, who knows, you may be riding in one of the vehicles that deposited soldiers on the beaches of Normandy on D-Day. Or at least you can imagine that for a moment. Wisconsin Dells is Wisconsin's top tourist destination, so there are many, many other things to see and do, such as water shows, go carts, and all the standard tourist town fare such as haunted houses, oddball museums like Ripley's Believe It or Not, and tourist shops filled with moccasins, woodsy souvenirs, magnets, postcards, and a wide selection of tee shirts. Between the waterparks and the other tourist attractions the city draws several million visitors a year.

WISCONSIN RAPIDS: Paper City

The first paper mill in Wisconsin Rapids opened in 1888. The largest one was built in 1904 and was an early user of electricity for its machines. That mill, which was the city's largest employer, closed just a few years ago, devastating the city and sending the Paper City nickname into oblivion. The paper industry was a huge part of

Wisconsin Rapids' history and identity. In fact, the big mill was built several years before the towns on both sides of the river decided to join forces and become what is now the city of Wisconsin Rapids. The plant is still sitting idle, but it is for sale, giving some citizens the hope that it may someday reopen, the jobs will come back, and the name Paper City will be a proud nickname again.

WOODMAN: The Dinky's Last Stop

Although Woodman bills itself as the Dinky's last stop, there is a four-car train called the Dinky that now resides in Fennimore, but it is not the one that used to travel between the two towns. The Dinky's real last stop is in Nevada where it was transported and is on display in a city park in the town of Pioche. The Dinky was a narrow-gauge train that used to run twice a day between Fennimore and Woodman and was the longest running narrow gauge railroad in the state's history. The Dinky's last official stop was at Woodman in 1926 after 48 years of service. While the train was running, Woodman was at the end of the line before returning back to Fennimore, so the train had to turn around on a turntable to go back the other way. The town was the last stop daily while the train ran and also the last stop when the railroad decided to end the line. Today there is a general store called the Dinky General Store and there is the Dinky Trail, a bike trail that runs on highways that are closest to where the railroad tracks used to be. Bikes can be rented at the Dinky General Store or at the Fennimore Railroad Historical Society Museum and returned at the other end of the trail at either location.

WOODRUFF: Home of the World's Biggest Penny

Yet another of Wisconsin's many large folk sculptures is the world's largest penny. Most of these folk sculptures are cast in fiberglass, or built with rocks, glass, seashells, and more. The penny in Woodruff is a concrete rendition of a Lincoln head penny with a year date of 1953. The penny is ten feet across and weighs over 17,000 pounds. It commemorates a fund-raising effort by the community to collect money to build a local hospital. The drive was spearheaded by Dr. Kate Pelham Newcomb, who encouraged children to save pennies to help build the hospital, while also soliciting money from several other sources, including the community's adults. After nationwide news coverage of the effort, donations came in from all over the country and the hospital was built. In about four moths 1.7 million pennies had been collected and thousands of people attended a Million Penny Parade to celebrate the achievement. The town has a museum honoring Dr. Kate and local history through a number of exhibits.

BIBLIOGRAPHY

For further reading or information, the following sources may prove useful.

BOOKS:
Minnich, Jerry (general editor). *The Wisconsin Almanac.* (Madison, WI: North Country Press, 1989)
Will, Tracy. *Wisconsin.* (Oakland, CA: Fodor's Travel Publications, 1994)
Feldman, Michael & Cook, Diana. *Wisconsin Curiosities* (Globe Pequot Press, 2004)
Wisconsin Legislative Reference Bureau. *Wisconsin Blue Book, 2021-2022* (Madison, WI; Department of Administration, 2021)

INTERNET: The following web sites proved useful in compiling this book. Please note some may no longer be active.

Albany: vil.albany.wi.us; lsrwa.org
Algoma: algoma.org
American Birkebeiner (Cable): birkie.com
Angel Museum, The (Beloit): angelmuseum.com
Appleton: jefflindsay.com/Appleton.html
Baraboo: baraboo.com
Bayfield: bayfield.org
Belgium: village.belgium.wi.us
Belleville: belleville-wi.com
Beloit: beloitwi.com
Benton: ci.benton.wi.us/
Berlin: berlinareahistoricalsociety.com; cityofberlin.net
Birchwood: birchwoodwi.com
Bloomer: win.bright.net/~chamber
Bonduel: villageofbonduel.com
Boscobel: boscobelwisconsin.com
Boulder Junction: boulderjct.org
Boyceville: boycevillewi.com
Brodhead: brodnet.com/cityofbrodhead
Burlington: burlington-wi.com
Cable: cable4fun.com

Cashton: bikesandberries.com/cashton.html
Cassville: cassville.org
Chequamegon Fat Tire Festival (Cable): cheqfattire.com
Chippewa Valley (Augusta): eauclaire-info.com
Circus World Museum (Baraboo): circusworldmuseum.com
Colby: clark-cty-wi.org/colby.htm
Columbus: www.columbuswichamber.com
Cumberland: cumberland-wisconsin.com
Delavan: ci.delavan.wi.us
Eau Claire: visiteauclaire.com
Eagle River: eagle-river.com
Ellsworth: ellsworthchamber.com
Experimental Aircraft Association (Oshkosh): eaa.org
Fennimore: www.fennimore.com
Fremont: www.fremontwis.com; travelfremontwi.org
Germantown: germantownchamber.org
Grandview (Hollandale): nicksgrandview.com
Grant County (Dickeyville): grantcounty.org
Grantsburg: grantsburgareahistoricalsociety.weebly.com
Green Lake: cityofgreenlake.com
Gygax Memorial (Lake Geneva): www.gygaxmemorialfund.org
Hayward: haywardareachamber.com; haywardlakes.com
Hazel Green: villageofhazelgreen.org
Holy Hill (Hubertus): holyhill.com
Horicon Marsh (Dodge County):
dnr.state.wi.us/org/land/wildlife/reclands/horicon/
International Clown Hall of Fame (Baraboo): theclownmuseum.org
Iron River: iracc.com
Kinstone: kinstonecircle.com
Lafayette County (Argyle, Belmont, Benton, Shullsburg):
wicip.uwplatt.edu/lafayette
La Follette, Robert (Argyle): informationplease.com
Lake Superior Big Top Chautauqua (Bayfield): bigtop.org
Lone Rock: villageoflonerock-wi.gov
Marshfield: centralwisconsinstatefair.com
Mercer: mercercc.com
New Glarus: newglarus-wi.com
Oconto: cityofoconto.com, ocontocounty.org;
ocontoareachamber.com

Sauk City: saukcity.net
Spelling Capital (Bonduel): madison.com/small-acts-can-nurture-success/article_4806b2fa-5405-5a58-ba2b-c65c7bad7585.html
Superior: worldofaccordions.org
Tomah: tomahwisconsin.com
Wisconsin Cranberries (Warrens): wiscran.org
Waupun: cityofwaupun.org
Winneconne: sovereignstateofwinneconne.com
Wisconsin Dells: wisdells.com
Wisconsin Rapids: visitwisrapids.com
General Sites:
    Atlas Obscura: atlastobscura.com
    Explore Wisconsin.com: explorewisconsin.com
    Lower Sugar River Watershed Association: lsrwa.org
    Roadside America: roadsideamerica.com
    Travel Wisconsin: travelwisconsin.com
    Weird Wisconsin: weird-wi.com
    Wisconsin Department of Tourism: tourism.state.wi.us
    Wisconsin Electronic Reader: library.wisc.edu/etext/WIReader
    Wistravel dot com: wistravel.com
    World's Largest Roadside Attractions:
infomagic.com/~martince/index.htm

MISCELLANEOUS:

Wisconsin has many historical markers which helped in putting this volume together. Many travel brochures, guidebooks, maps, etc. from the State of Wisconsin and various towns, cities, and counties were also consulted. These can generally be obtained from any city or county department of tourism, convention and visitors' bureau, or Chamber of Commerce. For much of the book, Internet searches were done and multiple sites were found which shared the same or similar information. In cases where there were conflicting "facts," neither was used without verification from additional sources.

APPENDIX

Many Wisconsin towns are known as the birthplace, hometown, or occasional residence of famous or important people. This list includes those who are nationally or internationally well-known rather than locally or regionally. It is a sampling and does not represent every famous or important person from the state.

Jim Abrahams, movie director—Shorewood
Stephen Ambrose, historian—Whitewater
Alan Ameche, football player—Kenosha
Don Ameche, actor—Kenosha
Roy Chapman Andrews, naturalist—Beloit
Walter Annenberg, publisher—Milwaukee
Antler, poet—Wauwatosa
Les Aspin, Congressperson/Secretary of Defense—Milwaukee
Victor Berger, Congressperson—Milwaukee
Rocky Bleier, football player—Appleton
Richard Bong, air ace—Poplar
Jerome Case, founder of J. I. Case—Racine
Carrie Catt, suffragist—Ripon
Liz Cheney, Congressperson—Madison
Kathryn Clarenbach, co-founder and first chair of the National Organization for Women—Sparta
Ellen Corby, actor—Racine
Craig Counsell, baseball player/manager—Whitefish Bay
Seymour Cray, supercomputer designer—Chippewa Falls
Willem DaFoe, actor—Appleton
Jeffrey Dahmer, serial killer—Milwaukee
Tyne Daly, actor—Madison
Arthur Davidson, co-founder of Harley-Davidson—Milwaukee
August Derleth, author/publisher—Sauk City
Dan Devine, football coach—Augusta
Jeanne Dixon, psychic—Medford
Lucius Fairchild, Civil War general/Governor—Madison
Chris Farley, actor/comedian—Madison
Edna Ferber, writer—Appleton
Lynn Fontanne, actor—Genesee Depot

Zona Gale, writer—Portage
Jim Gantner, baseball player—Eden
Hamlin Garland, writer—West Salem
Annie Laurie Gaylor, co-founder of the Freedom from Religion Foundation—Madison
Ed Gein, killer/grave robber—Plainfield
Bud Grant, football player/coach—Superior
Uta Hagen, actor/teacher—Madison
Suzy Favor Hamilton, Olympic runner—Stevens Point
William Harley, co-founder of Harley-Davidson—Milwaukee
Dan Harmon, writer/producer/actor—Milwaukee
Beth Heiden, Olympic speed skater/cyclist—Madison
Eric Heiden, Olympic speed skater—Madison
Phil Hellmuth, poker player—Madison
Woody Herman, musician/band leader—Milwaukee
Charlie Hill, standup comedian—Oneida
Elroy Hirsch, football player—Wausau
Joel Hodgson, writer/producer—Stevens Point
Harry Houdini, magician—Appleton
Al Jarreau, singer—Milwaukee
Mark Johnson, Olympian/hockey player/coach—Madison
Samuel Curtis Johnson, founder of S. C. Johnson Company—Racine
Colin Kaepernick, football player/activist—Milwaukee
George Kennan, diplomat/historian—Milwaukee
Matt Kenseth, NASCAR driver—Cambridge
Herb Kohl, co-founder of Kohl's/U. S. Senator—Milwaukee
John Michael Kohler, founder of Kohler Company—Sheboygan
Ron Kovic, soldier/writer—Ladysmith
Dave Krieg, football player—Iola
Harvey Kuenn, baseball player/manager—West Allis
Duane Kuiper, baseball player/sportscaster—Racine
Melvin Laird, Congressperson/Secretary of Defense—Marshfield
Robert LaFollette, politician—Primrose
Curly Lambeau, football player/coach—Green Bay
Tom Laughlin, actor—Milwaukee
William D. Leahy, U. S. Navy admiral—Ashland
Aldo Leopold, writer/naturalist—Baraboo
Liberace, pianist—West Allis
Jim Lovell, astronaut—Milwaukee

Allen Ludden, game show host—Mineral Point
Alfred Lunt, actor—Milwaukee
Douglas MacArthur, U. S. Army general—Milwaukee
Rick Majerus, basketball coach—Sheboygan
Fredric March, actor—Racine
Jackie Mason, comedian—Sheboygan
John Matuszak, football player—Oak Creek
Samuel Mazzuchelli, frontier missionary priest—Benton
Joseph McCarthy, U. S. Senator—Grand Chute
Golda Meir, Prime Minister of Israel—Milwaukee
Steve Miller, rock musician—Milwaukee
Billy Mitchell, U. S. Army general/father of the Air Force—West Allis
John Muir, environmentalist—Portage
Gaylord Nelson, Governor/U. S. Senator/Earth Day founder—Clear Lake
Lorine Niedecker, poet—Fort Atkinson
John Nichols, journalist—Union Grove
Andy North, golfer—Thorp
Sterling North, writer—Edgerton
Pat O'Brien, actor—Milwaukee
Georgia O'Keefe, painter—Sun Prairie
Danica Patrick, racecar driver—Beloit
Les Paul, musician/inventor—Waukesha
Charlotte Rae, actor—Milwaukee
William Rehnquist, Supreme Court Chief Justice—Milwaukee
Gena Rowlands, actor—Cambria
Mark Ruffalo, actor—Kenosha
Paul Ryan, politician/Speaker of the House—Janesville
Carl Schurz, politician/Secretary of the Interior—Watertown
Margarethe Schurz, kindergarten founder—Watertown
Bud Selig, baseball team owner/baseball commissioner—Milwaukee
Tony Shalhoub, actor—Green Bay
Christopher Sholes, inventor of the typewriter—Milwaukee
Deke Slayton, astronaut—Sparta
Tom Snyder, newscaster/talk show host—Milwaukee
Zack Snyder, movie director—Green Bay
Harry Steenbock, biochemist—Charlestown
Steve Stricker, golfer—Edgerton

Bob Suter, hockey player—Madison
Gary Suter, hockey player—Madison
James Thompson, biologist/stem cell researcher—Madison
Tommy Thompson, politician/Secretary of Health and Human
Services—Elroy
Fuzzy Thurston, football player—Altoona
Spencer Tracy, actor—Milwaukee
Daniel J. Travanti, actor—Kenosha
Dick Trickle, racecar driver—Wisconsin Rapids
Frederick Jackson Turner, historian—Portage
Bob Uecker, baseball player/announcer—Milwaukee
Butch Vig, musician/producer—Viroqua
J. J. Watt, football player—Pewaukee
Peter Weller, actor—Stevens Point
Orson Welles, actor/writer/director—Kenosha
Bradley Whitford, actor—Madison
Bob Wickman, baseball pitcher—Green Bay
Ella Wheeler Wilcox, poet—Johnstown
Gene Wilder, actor—Milwaukee
Laura Ingalls Wilder, writer—Pepin
Thornton Wilder, playwright—Madison
T. Harry Williams, historian—Hazel Green
Frank Lloyd Wright, architect—Richland Center
Joseph Zimmerman, inventor of the answering machine--Kenosha
David Zucker, writer/producer/director—Milwaukee
Jerry Zucker, writer/producer/director—Milwaukee

Several of Wisconsin's state symbols were mentioned in this book. There are more than one might think. Below is a list of all of the official state symbols as of 2023:

State Animal: Badger
State Ballad: "Oh, Wisconsin, Land of My Dreams"
State Beverage: Milk
State Bird: Robin
State Coat of Arms: A shield with four fields representing agriculture, mining, manufacturing, and navigation; a small shield in the middle represents the United States and Wisconsin's loyalty to it; the figures on both sides of the large shield represent labor on water

and land (sailor and yeoman); above the shield is a badger and the state moto, Forward. At the bottom is a horn of plenty representing prosperity and abundance next to 13 ingots representing mineral wealth and the original 13 colonies of the United States.
State Dairy Product: Cheese
State Dance: Polka
State Dog: American water spaniel
State Domesticated Animal: Dairy cow
State Fish: Muskellunge
State Flag: Blue background with the state coat of arms at center, the word "Wisconsin" above it and the date "1848" below it.
State Flower: Wood violet
State Fossil: Trilobite
State Fruit: Cranberry
State Grain: Corn
State Herb: Ginseng
State Insect: Honeybee
State Mineral: Galena
State Motto: Forward
State Pastry: Kringle
State Rock: Red granite
State Seal: The great seal is the state coat of arms with the words "Great Seal of the State of Wisconsin" at the top and a line of 13 stars representing the original American colonies.
State Slogan: America's Dairyland
State Soil: Antigo silt loam
State Song: "On Wisconsin"
State Symbol of Peace: Mourning dove
State Tartan: 44 muted blue threads, 6 scarlet, 4 muted blue 6 gray, 28 black, 40 dark green, 4 dark yellow, 40 dark green, 28 black, 22 muted blue, and 12 dark brown (half sett with full count at the pivots)
State Tree: Sugar maple
State Waltz: "The Wisconsin Waltz"
State Wildlife Animal: White-tailed deer

ABOUT THE AUTHOR

Callen Harty is the author of 24 produced plays, about 50 monologues, and numerous articles, essays, and poems that have been published in various print and online sites. His monologues for the Wisconsin Veterans Museum's annual cemetery tour, *Talking Spirits*, won awards from the Wisconsin Historical Society and the American Association of State and Local History. He is a member of the Wisconsin Writers Association, Wisconsin Fellowship of Poets, and a lifetime member of Broom Street Theater. Originally from Shullsburg, Wisconsin, he now lives in Monona, Wisconsin with his partner, Brian, and several pets.

His previous books are *My Queer Life*, a collection of writings from 30 years as an LGBT activist; *Empty Playground: A Survivor's Story*, a memoir about surviving childhood sexual abuse; *Invisible Boy*, an autobiographical play about child abuse; *The Stronger Pull*, a memoir about coming out in small town Wisconsin; *The Townsend Brothers of Shullsburg, Wisconsin*, a genealogical book about his great-great-grandfather and other ancestors; *A Wake*, a play about a Wisconsin family holding an old-fashioned Irish wake in their home; *Breathe Passion: Remembering the Wisconsin Uprising*, a collection of essays and photographs from a year of protests against the legislative agenda of Governor Scott Walker; *Compendium*, his first book of poetry; *A Full Heart*, a collection of personal essays; and a companion volume, *Bleeding Heart*, a collection of political essays.

For information on his books and other work, visit callenharty.com or follow him on his Facebook author page or Goodreads.